MORE BOOKS FRОM THE SAGER GROUP

Students Write the Darnedest Things:
Gaffes, Goofs, Blunders and Unintended
Wisdom from Actual College Papers
by Pamela Hill Nettleton, PhD

Into the River of Angels: A Novel
by George Wolfe

Meeting Mozart: A Novel Drawn from the Secret
Diaries of Lorenzo Da Ponte
by Howard Jay Smith

Notes from the Road: A Filmmaker's Journey through American
by Robert Mugge

Going Home to Die No More:
A True Kentucky Story about a Train Robbery and a
Hanging after the Civil War
by Russ Witcher

The Deadliest Man Alive:
Count Dante, The Mob and the War for American Martial Arts
by Benji Feldheim

Lifeboat No. 8: Surviving the Titanic
by Elizabeth Kaye

The Pope of Pot: And Other True Stories of Marijuana
and Related High Jinks
by Mike Sager

See our entire library at TheSagerGroup.net

A CALL

WISDOM ON INVESTMENT, CAREER AND LIFE FROM

FROM

DR. C. TERRENCE DOLAN, THE MOST SUCCESSFUL

EXPERIENCE

TRAILBLAZER YOU'VE NEVER HEARD ABOUT

RORY LINK

A Call from Experience: Wisdom on Investment, Career and Life from Dr. C. Terrence Dolan, The Most Successful Trailblazer You've Never Heard About
Copyright © Rory Link

Published in the United States of America.

Cover and Interior Designed by Siori Kitajima, PatternBased.com

Cataloging-in-Publication data for this book is available from the Library of Congress
ISBN-13:
eBook: 978-1-958861-18-9
Paperback: 978-1-958861-19-6

Published by The Sager Group LLC
(TheSagerGroup.net)

A CALL

WISDOM ON INVESTMENT, CAREER AND LIFE FROM

FROM

DR. C. TERRENCE DOLAN, THE MOST SUCCESSFUL

EXPERIENCE

TRAILBLAZER YOU'VE NEVER HEARD ABOUT

RORY LINK

THE SAGER GROUP

Artifex Te Adiuva

CONTENTS

OPENING COMMENTS

WHAT IS THIS

Many of the world's greatest minds have a hard time articulating their philosophies when asked about them directly. These philosophies are dynamic and cover far more ground than can possibly be stuffed into a quick answer to a spontaneous question. However, by asking detailed questions over time, and by watching how someone thinks and acts in diverse situations, it's possible to elicit their winning strategy successfully. Although I never got accepted into medical school, I felt like a doctor carefully dissecting the mind and thought process of Dr. C. Terrence Dolan, M.D., whom I will refer to respectfully as "Terry" for the rest of this book. You probably don't recognize the name, but there is a 33 percent chance you and your healthcare provider benefit from the computer-based laboratory information system he co-created decades ago, which is used by one-third of U.S. hospitals and clinical laboratories around the world. I have put this trailblazer's extraordinary life under a microscope to extract key insights that will allow myself and others to mirror his success.

You are about to tap into the raw, on-going conversations that took place over the past five years between myself, a twenty-three-year-old recent college graduate in search of direction, and Terry, an eighty-five-year-old established giant in multiple industries, including medicine, technology, real estate, and oil, to name a few, who was generous enough to share the wisdom he gained from his experience.

The information in the following pages will serve as a time machine, allowing you to travel back through the well-documented history of Terry Dolan to see how he both developed and continues to use his philosophy to create new innovations and great wealth. This book is an opportunity to learn powerful lessons without having to spend decades in the field. It's a road map of how to cultivate long-lasting relationships, develop profitable businesses and investments regardless of your professional background, and design your ideal lifestyle just like the 0.1 percent.

This book can also be thought of as a filter, allowing you to step into the mind and see, through the eyes of someone who has victoriously overcome diverse economic and life challenges, what is worthy of your time and energy, and what should be left behind. Terry does the heavy lifting by skipping over the unimportant minutia and highlighting only the most important insights that have led to abundance in his life. It makes no sense to reinvent the wheel. Instead, learn how the wheel works from someone who is successfully spinning it.

A stress-tested philosophy is the easiest type to deem credible because it's backed by tangible results. It felt nice to listen to someone I knew I could trust because I could see the long-term return on investment of his principles. I knew what I was going to get, and so will you.

I find it amusing when self-proclaimed "gurus" or internet bloggers, with only a drop of experience, confidently market their "successful tips and tricks," claiming to have the keys to life and wealth, eager to sell those keys to anyone with two ears and a wallet. I've personally fallen for their traps numerous times. It's not only a spirit crushing affair, but something that breaks trust, making it hard to believe anyone's advice. Who has credibility? Thanks to the internet, anyone can emit noise into the world. In some ways it's empowering, but it can also have the effect of drowning out truly authentic individuals. What makes the rare messages like this one even harder to come by is the fact that some of the most experienced professionals refrain from advertising their success since it offers diminishing returns on their time investment. Advertising their success can also put an unnecessary target on their back. These individuals aren't desperate for a quick buck or fame. Their achievements speak for themselves. As the saying goes, the smartest, or perhaps the most successful, one in the room says nothing at all. However, I've come to learn that if you reach out to these experts and show your genuine interest in learning their philosophy, you might just be lucky enough to see them pull back the curtains and reveal their most powerful secrets. These secrets are the treasures that await you in this book.

Admittedly, after our first few conversations, I was hesitant about whether Terry was regurgitating popular ideas he'd read in some trendy *New York Times* best sellers or from genuine personal experience. I revealed to him my early suspicions and asked if he was an avid reader of self-help books. He chuckled. "The ups and downs of my life experience over the past eight and a half decades taught me how to help myself," he said. "I didn't find all the answers in print." I was baffled at how he could offer such insightful ideas without reading them somewhere else. I now realize that Terry learned these concepts from the merciless teacher that is experience, earned by overcoming a rigorous curriculum of trial and error, supplemented by the conversations with and knowledge gained from other professionals who had already achieved the degree of success he desired. It was only after hearing his real-life stories, the background that led him to adopt these key principles, that I realized the lessons he was teaching were authentic. This book is not theory; it's information derived from the defeats and victories of everyday life. This is a philosophy with battle scars and history. Most importantly, this is the story of a life being well lived.

BENEFITS AND MAIN OBJECTIVES

The main benefit of this book is that it's written explicitly from a collection of ultra successful personal experiences. An integration of what Terry failed at, overcame, and the tips and tricks he learned over eighty-five years of winning the game of life. No one can buy experience. It's possible to appear experienced—in other words, fake it till you make it—but the most valuable wisdom can only be earned through time in the game. This time is what separates Terry from the masses. He's a warrior who has been in the ring longer than anyone else.

So, what was Terry able to manifest living by this philosophy? He earned his medical degree from Creighton University, graduating first in his class, received his Pathology specialty at the Mayo Clinic, and is currently board certified in three areas. He has served as an instructor at the Mayo Clinic Medical School, a Clinical Professor of Pathology at the University of Oklahoma Medical School, and a member of the Board of Editors of the *American Journal of Clinical Pathology*. He has also served as president of the Oklahoma State Association of Pathologists.

He taught himself the basics of data processing and software programming to introduce automation and computer technology to the medical laboratory setting, becoming a lead developer of the Enterprise Data Warehouse, currently one of the most robust data warehouses in health care. With the help of three accountants, he went on to co-create the first software product, a Laboratory Information System (LIS), for a Fortune 500 electronic health record company, which was acquired by Oracle for $28 billion in June 2022.

In 1980, Terry co-founded, and is currently a managing partner of, a physician-owned professional corporation for a group of pathologists in Tulsa, Oklahoma. The following year he co-founded Regional Medical Laboratory, which has become one of the largest hospital-owned laboratories in the country, with over 650 employees that perform more than ten million clinical tests a year as of this writing. He served as both president and member of the Board of Directors of Regional Medical Laboratory until its sale to Labcorp in 2022. He's also currently a member of the board of the St. John Health System, under which Regional Medical Laboratory formerly operated.

As a result of his tremendous achievements, he was accepted as a member of the prestigious Royal College of Physicians in Ireland and, in 2018, was honored with the highest award offered by the Mayo Clinic for leadership in laboratory medicine. To this day, Terry continues to develop extensive methods of measuring laboratory performance, using informatics to leverage medical and management decisions in the clinical laboratory.

From lucrative stock holdings to oil exploration to over twenty years of owning a commercial real estate empire, being summoned to Saudi Arabia upon the king's request, and breeding over thirty pure bred registered Morgan horses on his ranch, Terry is clearly not a one-trick pony. Born to first-generation Irish-American parents, he embarked on this journey without any significant financial handouts or unique intellectual talents. He set off on foot with a worn backpack slung over his shoulder rather than in the leather driver's seat of a brand-new Mercedes gifted to him at birth.

At the same time, Terry has made enough money to understand that success extends far beyond the often overemphasized financial measure of wealth. If you were to ask him to elaborate, like I did, he would tell you that focusing on money won't net you lasting satisfaction. He'd probably add that working tirelessly to bring his three kids back together, all of them residing within the same city limits, continuing to live happily with his wife, rounding out a sixty-year marriage, and acquiring multiple vacation homes for getaways, reunions and to strengthen the ties of his entire extended family are amongst his greatest personal achievements. If this level of success is something you desire to emulate, then this is your handbook.

For most, it would be a miracle to accomplish just one of the feats mentioned above in a lifetime. The following pages will break down how he was able to perform all of them. This will gift you a mental framework adaptable to your own personal goals and unique life path so you might be able to do the same. You will learn about the mindset needed to start and run a profitable business, effective ways to invest, how to stand out as a leader, how to create a real estate dynasty, a new approach to grueling challenges, dealing with frustration, how to balance work and play, sustaining a long-term romantic relationship, and much more. Although there are many practical topics covered, understand that this isn't a step-by-step how to. The most useful knowledge is learned from direct personal experience or from the mouth of an expert who can teach from their own database of successful experience. The latter kind of knowledge is only as valuable as the action it inspires, and that is precisely our main goal. Action is the serum that will bring these passive words to life.

The first objective of this book is to supply you with actionable ideas that will facilitate incremental improvements to your own philosophy and daily activity. We want to help you exceed your goals. Slight changes lead to weighty sums. The second objective is to help you develop the mindset of jumping off the metaphorical cliff into the ocean of new experience despite uncertainty and fear. In other words, the intention of this book is to create a paradigm shift in how you approach the learning process and novel challenges. Experience is the key word here. The third and final objective of this book is to combat the stress rooted in the popular belief that success requires complete plans, a clear direction, or special ability from the start. News flash: there is no prerequisite or a hell of a lot you need to start with to be successful. You don't need to emerge a genius straight out of the womb with your entire life plan mapped out. Terry's story is proof. Most importantly, you don't have to pigeonhole yourself in one college major or remain shackled to your primary occupation. Overcoming industry barriers is Terry's specialty.

My hope in authoring this work is to touch inquisitive people like myself, who have a passionate curiosity to learn, and who are relentlessly searching for actionable and authentic principles to better navigate the complex world around them. This book is also meant for individuals who have plateaued and desire some fresh insight to unleash their untapped potential. Forward progress in your personal development journey will make this book a success for all of us. Enjoy.

FORMAT

My primary role is to translate Terry's story in a manner that is both entertaining and accurate. I'm the means of transporting this information, which has been so integral to my own development, to others who might benefit as well. I've put an enormous emphasis on preserving his actual responses, keeping them raw and untouched, minus a few tweaks along the way to maintain a coherent flow. With that said, this information isn't riddled with complex formulas or definitions. In fact, it was a straightforward dictation because Terry understood he was talking to someone in their early twenties. Impractical stodgy language would've gone to the equivalent of my mind's recycling bin, straight out the right ear. There's no fluff, all meat.

The following are lessons Terry felt were important enough to mention when I picked apart his success, starting with the story of his incredible career in Part One; powerful business insights, which will be discussed in Part Two; his personal investment approach, which will be covered in Part Three; a breakdown of how to build a lucrative commercial real estate portfolio in Part Four; and lifestyle advice he picked up along the journey packed into Part Five. Every idea in this book might not be of direct interest to you. However, if you're interested in improving the financial and relational aspects of your life, I'd bet that at least one will be.

With this unique format, you are now able to tap into our private conversations and use them to catapult yourself to a higher state of living. Without this notation, I do not believe these valuable insights would have spread beyond the confines of Terry's family tree. If you are listening to the audio format of this book, work out, walk the dog, watch the dog work out, or sprawl out on a lawn chair with the print version and digest this accumulation of experience, thoughts, and ideas that have resulted in millions of dollars, long-lasting relationships, and a life lived in style. This book is meant to be savored.

PREFACE

PREFACE

t was a humid spring evening in Tulsa the first time we met in person. He was surprisingly tall, towering over my five-foot-nine frame at six foot two, but he had a calming presence and a smile that put us on the same level. He had a full head of silky hair the color of snow and plate-sized hands in line with the Irish roots of his ancestors. His blue jean slacks emanated simplicity, and the plaid button-down shirt he was wearing lacked even the slightest resemblance to flashy designer apparel. Aside from the ring on his finger, there was no gold jewelry on his body. That's what a million-aire looks like, huh? I didn't understand, until he cracked open a Guinness for each of us, invited me to sit at the rustic circular table, and started to engage with me, that there was more to this man than well-washed jeans and a good ol' boy affect.

Although I'm sure he had polarizing emotions, I never saw them. During my visit, he was never angry, sad, or worried. He did laugh a lot, tilting his head back with deep breaths of joy erupting deep from his stomach and out through the beaming smile that was always glued to his face. What surprised me most was that he seemed so young, both in physical appearance and in how sharp his mind was. With a humble, quiet demeanor, he spent more time inquiring about my life than offering any insight into his own.

Let's rewind. I'll never forget the first *call* I had with Terry Dolan about five years ago. I was a starry-eyed eighteen-year-old finishing up my first year of college. Coincidentally, he was turning eighty-one. Leading up to our first conversation, I had tunnel vision from a lifelong dream of Division I soccer that, upon achievement, gave me more stress than satisfaction. A serious three-year relationship with my now ex-girlfriend was also imploding before my eyes. My net worth was negative, and I felt lost in every bucket of life. Everything

I thought I wanted turned out to be smoke and mirrors. It didn't feel right.

One steamy northern California night, during my freshman year at UC Davis, I was heading home on my silver Trek Mountain bike after a typical college house party. As I approached the Ryerson student housing commons on campus, my impatience, and the alcohol in my system, got the better of me. My brick dormitory building was situated on the opposite side of the empty four-lane road, with the nearest crosswalk fifty yards away in either direction. With a pinched face, I looked left, then right, then straight ahead at my cracked-open third-floor bedroom window. I figured I'd make my own shortcut, save a minute or two, and jump the curb. The moment the rubber tread of my front wheel made contact with that black gravel street, BOOM. The old tire exploded as the rusty metal chain under my foot snapped into pieces, sending my body flying headfirst toward the rocky pavement. Blackout.

I awoke in a dreamlike state at 6:00 am the following morning to the beeping of a heartbeat monitor in what felt like a depressing Hollywood movie, with my back flat on the hospital cot. I had a fractured orbital bone, the swelling around my face looked like I had gone the distance with Conor McGregor, and black asphalt still caked the peeling flesh on my cheek like makeup. That was after it was supposedly cleaned. The first responding officer later informed me that I had laid unconscious on the side of the street, with a fake Pennsylvania ID and a Coors Light stuffed into each pocket, until a good Samaritan drove by my seemingly lifeless shadow and dialed 9-1-1. That was the turning point. Something had to change.

Puzzled, I spent some time staring into the piercing fluorescent light on the ceiling of the hospital unit, wondering where it had all gone wrong. I had done all the right things that were supposed to make me feel like a success. I had gotten the blonde southern California girl, was recruited to play a Division I sport at a highly-ranked university, and had become the life of the party with a popular friend group. Only the feeling of success never came. I was left discouraged without any substantial career aspirations, or even a short-term plan, and now my health was taking a nosedive. Worst of all, I was still clutching on to some false hope that my current life philosophy, the one that had gotten me into this mess to begin with, would still somehow bring me to the top! There's nothing like a near-death experience to kick your ass back to reality.

My father had observed the extent of my dramatic decline, and I could see the worry in his eyes. It wasn't that I was lazy, dumb, or a negative person. On the contrary, I was a hard worker, a skilled student athlete, and I had an upbeat personality. The problem was I lacked direction. I was lost but couldn't face reality. My father offered a solution; to reach out to an older individual, who believe it or not, had more wisdom than I, or the baby-faced influencers in my Instagram feed, did. After hearing his impressive resume, and seeing as I was as close to rock bottom as one could get, I was sold on reaching out, but I was nervous. There was a huge generational gap at play. How could we ever relate?

It took me about a month to get around to dialing those ten digits. I was at an ex-girlfriend's house, of all places, locked upstairs in her room, pacing, anxiously waiting for the clock to read 4:00 pm. This was call number one. I had nothing to take notes with, no plan, and truthfully, I had no idea what I would say to this mysterious man. All I had were clammy hands and back sweat. That evening we began a transformative journey that continues to this day.

Learning from Terry has been a breath of fresh air throughout my young adult life, often a melting pot of noise and judgment. To every question I ask, he thinks before releasing an answer with a soothing flow. His voice is steady and lacks any sort of affliction. If he can't think of the best response off the top of his head, he's perfectly fine saying he needs to think about it. He always follows up. Terry doesn't tell you what you'd like to hear, but how he believes it to be based on his personal experience, regardless of whether it elicits a calming or unsettling effect. His life philosophy is a credible model in a world where authenticity is scarce, where everyone has their trigger finger on a hypothetical loaded submachine gun, able to fire off an endless barrage of mind-penetrating bullets of advice without any real experience to back their words. It can leave you dazed and confused in the pursuit of truth.

In each of our conversations, Terry was talking to me, but, in a sense, he was also talking to everyone in my extremely common predicament. Some calls were longer than others, some more detailed, some were about current events, and some were on his larger philosophy on careers, investment, and life. We covered a lot over the years. I humbly offer these insights to anyone who is motivated to improve their life with the help of someone with a successful public track record spanning decades, not an anonymous internet blogger. With that said, this story isn't about me, Terry, or anyone else. It's about you. Hopefully the message in the following pages can be an asset to your life and a useful example of what is possible.

I did eventually ask Terry what I could offer him in return for the helping hand he continued to extend in my direction. The time he spent reorienting me to the principles of success was money, and his rate wasn't cheap. He helped alter the trajectory of my life, in a sense saving my life, and that was worth more than everything I had. I was willing to give him all the change in my pocket. Terry gave the same simple response every time I asked. He urged me to pass on any helpful guidance I had received to others in a similar dark situation. To be clear, he never had any intention of making our one-on-one conversations public. For months, I procrastinated telling him I was organizing my personal notes into this book, as he's extremely private about his life and a humble individual by nature. He might just be the most successful trailblazer you've never heard about. Until now, of course. Clearly, fame was never one of his goals, but he did inspire me to act. This is my way, in your words, Terry, of "paying it forward".

As I write this, I'm a recent college graduate, and, looking back, I can see just how dramatically he helped me find my way, little by little, every call. Being one of the few individuals to have internalized this philosophy, direct from the source, I can tell you that my improvement has been quite dramatic. My troubled past self has become a speed bump along the road, instead of a dead end. I'm not yet where I need to be, but I'm now moving in the right direction. Terry's advice was a huge influence on my 180-degree turnaround. His teaching helped me form a positive mindset that has facilitated even further growth.

Here's the kicker. It took me several years of consistent interviews and dedicated research to elicit his extraordinary life strategy. This book has condensed that process into a matter of hours. As you flip this page, you will embark on a new journey, and there are no limits to where you can go. Don't forget; now it's on you to pay it forward. It's time to pick up and answer a call from experience. Welcome to the conversation.

PART ONE
WHERE IT ALL STARTED

ONE
INCREDIBLE OPPORTUNITY & SWIFT ACTION

"You can never cross the ocean until you have the courage to lose sight of the shore." – Christopher Columbus

"People who are unable to motivate themselves must be content with mediocrity, no matter how impressive their other talents." – Andrew Carnegie

"A journey of a thousand miles begins with one simple step." – Lao Tzu

NO GIANT OF INTELLECTUAL OR FINANCIAL CAPITAL

D r. Terrence Dolan: Growing up I didn't have much, but I did have two hard-working parents that taught me the principles of right and wrong. My father was a pharmacist. He was a wise man that put in long hours and tried not to make any waves. My mother, on the other hand, only had a high school education, but she was one of the smartest people I've ever been around. She had such good intuition and could always anticipate what the hell I was thinking. Occasionally, Pop would put the foot down, but his five-foot-one wife did most of the decision making. Mom was the driving force.

My mother had an ear infection when she was younger, and even with hearing aids, she was practically deaf in both ears. To get around this acute impediment she taught my older sister, Jean, and I to repeat what was said in group conversations. We were her ears. When she was home alone, she always had a dog by her side that would bolt to the phone or door when someone was ringing or knocking. Dogs looked out for her; I think they had a sense that she needed them. Be that as it may, she never complained about her impairment and worked arduously to maneuver through every challenge that resulted from it. Although she became amazingly perceptive, she would rarely venture out in public because of her handicap. My father was a quiet man who didn't mind being a homebody, so we had lots of family time together when I was young. My parents were pleased with my sister and I, for the most part.

I was a challenging student growing up. My mother's goal was to straighten me out. This proved to be a difficult task; I guess I had some of her stubborn genes. One scorching Midwest spring she got ahold of my failing grade school report card. She was so frustrated with what she saw that she stuck me out on the front porch in a pink dress for half the day. It didn't faze me one bit. Regardless of what I did, she always worked with me. Various grade school and high school teachers also contributed to my cause. I once took a math exam in grade seven, and my teacher, who doubled as a nun, approached me on the playground afterwards to ask me what I thought I got on it. I figured zero would be one of the integers in that figure. When she revealed that I had gotten my first perfect score I was absolutely dumbfounded. She added, "I have a feeling you have a lot more capability than you're letting on." That got my wheels turning. When I was young, I lacked self-confidence, but slowly certain people in my life drew it out of me. Their collective support kept my head above water long enough for me to learn how to swim.

There was nothing abnormal about my high school years. The subjects of chasing girls and enjoying parties took precedent over the others. I enjoyed it maybe a little too much at times. However, by my sixteenth birthday I had taken a part-time job at the local pharmacy, a block away from my home, working every weekend, and on some occasions, in the evening during the week. This helped me derive self-confidence from my ability to work hard. Eventually, I got it together in high school.

There is a saying that Jewish and Irish mothers are exactly the same. That they basically rule the roost with an iron fist. I couldn't have said it any better. Toward the end of my senior year, with college admissions looming, my mother asked me about my career path. By this point, I had already transformed my identity into that of a hard worker, but I still lacked any inkling of what I wanted to pursue long term. She pushed me in a direction, saying, "Your father was always able to make a living through the Depression, so you're going to start in pharmacy like he did. You can figure the rest out later." End of conversation. My mother was a driving force. She knew more than I did at the time, and because I felt she had my best intentions at heart, I took a stab at it.

I enrolled in the University of Kansas City Pharmacy School with the class of 1954. As I invested more of my time and effort into the study of medicine, I started leaning toward an emphasis in pharmacology, which is the study of the interaction of drugs within the human body. I revealed my master plan to the department chairman of pharmacy. He had his Ph.D., but told me not to bother getting one, and instead pushed me to get a Doctor of Medicine, or M.D., which, in his exact words, "would give me a ticket to do virtually anything." He instructed, "You're young enough to get your M.D. and still have ample time move in another direction if you so desire in the future. Create the foundation, then build the house." At a young age I opened my mind and ears to people who had more experience than I did, those who had been to the promised land, and that was quite possibly the smartest thing I ever did. This department chairman was right, because with an M.D. ticket in hand, you have access to almost any route in healthcare. I made up my mind to pursue medical school, even though I would have to take an additional semester of physics courses before I applied. The first milestone was to complete the rest of my undergraduate education.

I completely underestimated how difficult the path to becoming a doctor would be. It didn't take me long to figure out that it would demand every ounce of my energy. In those days, pharmacy was a four-year undergraduate degree, but due to the number of hours it required to complete, the school had to extend the program to five years shortly after I finished. Free time was almost nonexistent for me because, on top of my undergraduate coursework, I also continued to work various low-level positions at the local pharmacy store. I chose to work primarily because I needed the cash, but it turned out to be a blessing in more ways than one. This disciplined schedule kept me from getting distracted and on track to reach my goals.

As the end of my senior year approached, I set my sights on joining a larger regional drug store chain in my off hours. They always had an appetite for new pharmacists, and with over sixty stores across the Midwest, I knew I could pick up shifts over holiday breaks if I were to visit home from an out-of-state medical school in the future. The problem was I had to pass the state of Missouri board exam first. Fortunately, I was able to expedite the process and take the test a little early since I had accumulated enough prior experience as an assistant at my local pharmacy. I graduated with a bachelor of pharmacy in the first half of May, took the state board exam the first half of June, and was stuck on the evening shift at Katz Drug Store a week or two before I got my results back. For the conclusion of my undergraduate senior year, I played the role of student by day and practicing pharmacist by night.

Most of the company's seasoned professionals refused to work in the high-crime-rate submarkets of Kansas City out of concern for their safety. My arrival turned out to be their golden solution. I was stationed on the front lines servicing customers over the counter as a rookie. I had the pleasure of working in some of the toughest neighborhoods in the region, shady places where you had to be wary of addicts trying to rob you for narcotics. Although I wasn't the most physical guy, I was six foot two with thick jet-black hair and looked more intimidating than I was. I knew this position wasn't going to be permanent, and I was on a fast track, planning to leave for medical school by the coming fall, so nothing was going to deter me.

The grind seemed endless, but it allowed me to pay my way through Creighton University Medical School in Omaha, Nebraska, from 1958 to 1962. I was on the clock at Katz Drug Store for the entirety of my freshman and sophomore summers, in addition to whenever I visited home for the holidays. During the school year I was also the only pharmacist on shift at one of Creighton's busiest hospital pharmacies through Sunday evening. Between work and studying, aside from a few belligerent nights at the frat house, my social life was, once again, nonexistent.

In medical school, the professors try to sort out their students, to see if they have the wherewithal to survive a tremendous amount of stress. With the kind of pressure you are subjected to, you either survive it or you don't, and even if you do, you'll find yourself at the edge of your breaking point. For example, our professors would periodically schedule exams every so many weeks, and during the final week leading up to the exam, they would intentionally double the course material we had to study. If they covered the first five chapters in class before the last week, they'd instruct us to read up to chapter ten by test day. As a freshman, I lived right across the street from an older junior friend of mine who was living at the frat house. One night I went over to vent about the craziness. He revealed that the professors were pressuring us for a reason, to see who could mentally handle the demands of the job. My friend explained that there would likely only be a few or no questions at all from the additional chapters. It was a bluff meant to psyche out the students who weren't totally confident in themselves. That's how my first exam played out, and after that, I never let myself worry too much. The other challenge you're dealing with, on top of that, is the fact that all the students in medical school were previously top performers in their undergraduate classes. So, you had the faculty trying to psyche you out while simultaneously competing with the cream of the crop. It was a son of a bitch, but I dug deeper into my position, fully committing to the challenge. One way or another, I was going to get through it.

Sophomore year was the gatekeeper, the toughest of the four. I had to spend an ungodly amount of time studying, something like seventy to eighty hours per week. Many of my peers couldn't handle the pressure and waved the white flag during year two. I was always empathetic to their situation because I could relate. At times I wondered why in the hell I was staying myself, but then I remembered I couldn't return home and face the wrath of my mother, so I didn't really have a choice. I knuckled down, and through the chaos, realized that work ethic is often a more valuable weapon than brains. I discovered my most powerful attribute.

After I emerged from the living hell of those first few medical school years, I could handle just about any kind of workload. Once, I was asked to present the two-page medical history and physical examination of a patient before our team discussed the diagnosis and how to approach the case later that week. The night before my presentation, I needed something to keep myself occupied, so I memorized the entire write-up before bed. The next day, I stood up in front of the group and presented the patient's complete history word for word. All wide eyes were glued on me. They didn't understand how long I'd been working at my limits. This work ethic paid off in dividends down the road, but at the time I couldn't see the full return on investment.

I never took my foot off the gas. In fact, I think I broke the gas pedal, finishing first in the class of 1962. When my mother came to the Creighton University Medical School graduation, she didn't know my rank. As I crossed the stage, she shot me a look that said, "I never doubted your capability." Earlier on, I didn't think I had the heart to do it. I'll never forget that look. Over my career, I've gotten to know some world-renowned businessmen and philanthropists. My five-foot-one driving force of a mother measured up to every single one of them. Once you hit your thirties you realize your parents are smarter than you thought. It takes life experience to understand.

Looking back, many people along the way taught me how to think through difficult situations. I took their suggestions to heart. This stage of my life solidified the principle of "learn from people who are more experienced than you" into my growing philosophy. I don't believe I was blessed with innate talent or natural ability. If anything, based on my early grade school development, I lacked them. However, I chose to work hard while drawing on those with more experience than I had to help channel my efforts in the right direction. Gradually, I found my way.

WHAT NOW

Upon my graduation from Creighton, I held a provisional license, but to become a board-certified physician, it was mandatory that I pass three exams in the state of Nebraska where I was living. I had already passed the first halfway through medical school, and I took the second by the end of my graduate education. Before I could even sit for the final test, I had to complete a year of practical experience out in the field.

I embarked on a twelve-month internship, rotating through several hospitals in Omaha that were associated with the university. This was my baptism by fire. I worked through sleepless nights and exhausting weekends, around eighty-five hours a week, almost exclusively between sundown and sunup, first in line to deal with an array of traumatic complications, from bleeding ulcers to congestive heart failure. I was exposed to a tremendous amount in a short period of time. St. Joseph, a semiprivate teaching hospital for Creighton University, was my home base. However, for the first six months of the internship, I was up to my elbows in blood at the challenging County Hospital, where I was temporarily assigned to the two toughest departments: the alcoholic's unit, where patients would go to get detoxed after having ten too many bottles of Thunderbird, and the emergency department, which dealt with trauma cases, including victims of gunshot and stab wounds.

County Hospital put me through the ringer, but it was one of the most valuable experiences in my life and career up to that point. Direct exposure to the somewhat controlled chaos stretched me around the clock. Particularly in the emergency department, when patients were rushed in with major trauma, it was a formidable task keeping them alive. For the first time I had to pronounce a patient who passed away on the cold operating table in front of me dead. I can also vividly recall a nightmarish conversation where I had to inform a pair of distraught parents that their sixteen-year-old didn't make it. I then had to explain to the hysterical adults what had happened with as much composure and tact as I could muster, even though my mind had since gone numb. I realized these were just some of the unavoidable, albeit less glamorous, parts of the job I signed up for. I invested all I had into perfecting my craft, and although I lost some, I kept many others alive that would've otherwise been six feet underground. Once I realized that a patient's survival was dependent on my performance, the naïve and unrealistic "cupcake phase" completely evaporated. However, if you love what you do, no challenge will be able to break you, and great responsibility will empower you.

County Hospital was always short on nursing staff, or, at the very least, there was an insufficient number of them to meet the overwhelming demand of the patients, so I'd often manage the entire alcoholic's unit with just one nurse. When the unit was maxed out, and it typically was, we'd get overwhelmed. I had to recruit patients who were farther along in their detox, coming out of delirium tremens—shaking caused by withdrawal—to help tend to the others who were in much more dismal shape. Many of the alcoholics were recurrent, so we got to know each other on a first name basis. A few would even ask where I was during my off shifts like a group of concerned friends. They didn't have anyone else left in their corner. I witnessed a lot of heart wrenching situations where senile individuals in shambles would be dumped on our doorstep by various family members. They depended on our staff to put their body and their life back together. I was a rookie at the time, and being understaffed was a rewarding experience because I absorbed a ton of practical knowledge. It was within the brick walls of County Hospital that I began to feel the deep satisfaction of making a direct positive impact on a patient's life.

In addition to the time I spent with the alcoholics and trauma patients, I also rotated through the tuberculosis unit for a few months. I was directly exposed to the highly infectious bacterium before the word COVID ever existed. Upon entering the rooms within the TB unit, with patients whom we knew with 100 percent certainty were positive, we took all the necessary precautions fully gowned up. However, it was extremely risky in the emergency department because, inevitably, we faced anonymous individuals who would stagger into the hospital intake room sneezing and coughing all over everyone. With just a flimsy paper mask as a shield, we dealt with them without knowing if they were infected or not. It was primarily these individuals, the question marks, that posed the greatest risk.

I ended up working so many hours that eventually County Hospital carved out a room for me to eat meals and catch a few hours of shut eye. It was often a matter of sleeping with one eye open because whenever I treated deathly ill patients, I'd personally stay up through the night to keep them alive. Other doctors would periodically rotate in to give me relief, but because I was single, I could afford to cover the extra emergency calls. I'd briefly pop into St. Joseph to change clothes, take a shower, and promptly head back through the revolving doors of the E.R. Throughout this internship, I consulted the most talented seniors at the health system to help me avoid catastrophic failures during the difficult cases I hadn't seen before. Between the experts I was able to learn from and the hours I was putting in, my clinical skills grew exponentially.

For the latter half of my internship at St. Joseph Hospital, I lived in a basement unit with the other house staff. As you can tell from the name, the hospital was run by a religious order, and the managing sisters got to know me well. Occasionally I would be summoned in the middle of the night for a code red when a patient's health was deteriorating. I'll never forget one situation where a nun aroused me at the crack of dawn by barking, "Doctor, we have a foreign bishop in the chancellery, and we need you to assist him in mass!" I used to retreat to that area of the hospital when I needed some air after an extra depressing case, specifically if I had lost someone, so I threw on a clean pair of whites, shook the bishop's hand, and assisted him with mass. I experienced a lot of unusual things over those twelve months, some more serious than others.

Although I learned a lot, I was also traumatized in the process. I hadn't seen what went on outside of the textbook, and my eyes were forcefully ripped open to the harsh reality of the field I was in. Traumatic injuries brought me back down to Earth. My love for medicine didn't fade, but I was hardened by what I witnessed. The job wasn't always attractive, but I kept reminding myself that this kind of experience, although ugly on the surface, was making me immensely more valuable to the industry. By the end of my internship, I had passed all the national and state board exams and was a fully licensed physician. My career was gaining traction, but I still had to choose a specialty, a decision I knew would dictate the rest of my career.

In 1963, the United States was midway through the Vietnam War, and every able-bodied male adult had to spend at least two years with the military by law. It was a mandatory requirement for us to sign up for the draft. I had gotten to know the chairman of the pathology department at Creighton University well during my time there. He always looked out for me. The chairman had previously spent most of his career in the U.S. Public Health Service and was familiar with their key contacts. He knew that I had to fulfill the two-year service requirement, so, upon discovering that an open residency slot was being offered by the U.S. Public Health Service, at their flagship hospital in Staten Island, New York, as part of their pathology training program, he did me a tremendous favor by helping to secure it. This program would satisfy the military requirement and give me a head start on my pathology specialty training. Most importantly, the war was dragging on, and it allowed me to swap out two years in Vietnam for two years in New York City. Which would you choose?

I originally planned to specialize in neurology, but the chairman changed my course. It was a favor that might've saved my life. I lost some close friends in Vietnam. Their MedEvac Bell UH-1 Iroquois helicopters, or "Hueys", were shot down, while others were lost on the battlefield. After seeing some of my colleagues deploy to Vietnam and not return, I recognized the true extent of what the chairman had done for me. It was once again a perfect example of listening to someone who was much more knowledgeable than I was. Immediately after completing my Omaha internship, I threw the few earthly belongings I owned in my car and motored to the

Big Apple, stopping only in Des Moines, Iowa, along the way to share one last dinner with my former medical school roommate, Denny McDonald, who I still share an occasional meal with sixty years later, before he deployed to Southeast Asia. Still, my residency on the East Coast would be no walk in the park either. I would also feel the touch of death.

This military-backed residency program rotated me through a couple different specialties. In the first year, I performed over fifty autopsies. Although I had already pronounced someone dead through my prior experience at County Hospital, dealing with lifeless human bodies still made me uneasy. Additionally, I wasn't thrilled about the autopsy rotation at first because performing one can invade a family's privacy. I really looked forward to saving someone's life or helping a patient survive *through* a situation. However, by the end of this rotation I ultimately considered performing an autopsy a privilege since what I learned from it could make the difference in extending someone else's life in the future. This experience taught me a tremendous amount about the disease process. During my second year of training, I was immersed in surgical pathology. This involved dealing with legions of various types and analyzing the microscopic tissue of tumors, both benign and malignant. My stint with the U.S. Public Health Service was all smooth sailing until January and February of my final year, which took place at sea.

Our crew of 150 sailors took off from Portland, Maine, tasked with patrolling the U.S. coastline in the North Atlantic. All our men were combat ready, fully armed, and prepared to defend the country. My job, as the only physician on the ship, was managing the health of the members of the Coast Guard. After boarding, I made my way to the officers' quarters to meet the crew. Right off the bat, the men told me that the doctor they had on board a year earlier, during the same season of miserable weather, got so sick he had to be airlifted to the nearest hospital in Greenland. I had never been to sea in my life, but I was young and invincible so I brushed off their stories, claiming, with all the confidence I could muster, "I can assure you; history is not going to repeat itself." I had no idea what I was getting into, and they laughed, thinking I was in over my head. They were probably right. No one in their right mind would've been out there in the wintertime, so we were all a little bit crazy.

Immediately after departing that frigid January, we sailed straight into a dark polar storm characterized by 150-mile-per-hour winds and forty-five-foot waves. We avoided icebergs by venturing further south, but if just one of the powerful blows from those behemoth waves had penetrated the wrong compartment of our ship, we'd never have been heard from again. We were fortunate, because when the sea did tear a hole and fill it with water, it was a non-critical compartment in the bow, and we were able to isolate the leak. I was concerned whether our rusty WWII Sea Tender, a ship that fueled other vessels during the war, would even hold together. It had been fitted with several improvements to make our voyage as safe as possible, but it wasn't designed for the North Atlantic or the force of that nautical storm.

We endured miserable conditions for over a month, and it beat the hell out of us. Only a few days of the entire trip were spared from stormy weather, and even then, it was a bitter and icy cold. Everyone was getting sick. Even the old salts had their heads over the railing. I was no exception. For the first few days of the voyage, I was green in the face. Luckily, the nausea would subside in the early morning so I could manage the sick bay, but by lunchtime I'd start to grow dizzy again. Eventually a strange equilibrium set in as my body adjusted to getting knocked around by the instability of the ship. Once the vertigo decreased, I hit a constant drowsy state where my brain was halfway through the process of shutting itself down, trying to catch a break after working on overdrive to process all the rapid sea changes. Be that as it may, I was fully committed to standing my ground. No matter how tough it got, there wasn't a chance in hell that I was ever going to allow myself to be ripped off that boat.

Nothing on our ship was easy. One of the sailors shuffled into sick bay with a sharp pain in the lower right quadrant of his abdomen, where the appendix is. I had the necessary equipment to do an operation, and although I had observed surgical cases where the appendix was removed in medical school, I wasn't trained as a surgeon, so it would've been risky. The standard operating procedure was to send the individual off to Greenland to be properly taken care of, but it was too windy for a helicopter to hover over our ship long enough to safely extract the patient. The man's excruciating pain had no regard for my limiting constraints. I poured antibiotics into him at extremely high-level doses through an IV and slapped hot packs on his side to settle down the appendix. That was sufficient to get him through the journey.

On another occasion, a sailor barged into sick bay with puss leaking out of his mouth. Good mornin'. Upon my own investigation, I discovered a dead, infected, and discolored front tooth. He had an infection in the root of that abscess tooth, which had broken through a little hole in his gum to drain. There was no doubt he experienced significant pain for days prior to our meeting, but he didn't care to alert anyone until the puss started to ooze. I figured the tooth had to come out, but I wasn't a dentist, so I called the U.S. Public Health Service's Boston-based oral surgeon for advice. The tooth was wedged in tight, and I was worried about snapping it off from the root because then the infection wouldn't adequately drain. The oral surgeon gave me a thirty-minute do-it-yourself tutorial on how to extract it, and then said, "You're it, you have to take it out, and good luck!" Click. To add to the stress of the situation, our second-in-command had to stay by my side in the sick bay while communicating with our captain on the bridge to steady the ship in between the enormous waves. Our boat had two gigantic propellers fitted with two motors on each, so it was a complicated and dangerous maneuver. I had a fraction of a minute, where I wasn't being thrown to the left or right, to execute. When you're it, you've got to do whatever it takes. I lashed the sailor hard to the table and injected him with a double dose of Demerol. I wanted him out cold. Here we go. During a lull between one of the monstrous waves, the ship settled, and my window of opportunity arrived. I had a hell of a time trying to pry that tooth out, but I pulled with all my might. I held that large bloody tooth in my pliers over my head like some twisted Olympic trophy.

I couldn't even take the simplest pleasures in life, like sleeping at night, for granted. Most of the sailors had swinging cots to secure them in place during the rough weather. I was in a state room, which had a stationary bed affixed to the wall. There was a fence-like rail on the opposite side that was supposed to prevent me from being yanked out of bed, but because the seas were so rugged, I constantly got thrown out, with various bruises to show for it. As a result, I had to wedge life preservers in between my body and the railing to keep myself from becoming a rag doll. I was constantly adapting.

Coast Guard ships are strategically placed at stations spanning the entire United States shoreline, fully armed with guns and missiles. Their primary objective is to defensively patrol the country's border from the water. We sailed up the North Atlantic through the Labrador Sea sandwiched between Greenland on the east and Newfoundland, Canada, on the west. No commercial ship would've taken the route we did in January due to the high probability and deadly risk of sinking. Admittedly, our crew was just as focused on surviving the barrage of liquid attacks from the ocean as it was on protecting the country.

There were two stations in our vicinity. Bravo was furthest north and impossible to get to in winter because it was surrounded with ice. We hit the end of our journey at Charlie, which saw no icebergs but bitter cold and tremendous wind. Upon our arrival at the ocean station, we battled through war drills and trained with the military vessel that was already based there. Besides the one we relieved, we didn't come across any other ships. Most of the time it was cloudy and gray. Occasionally, when the sky briefly cleared, we'd catch a glimpse of a huge commercial airplane buzzing overhead, transporting passengers from Europe to the States, I imagined. The only other thing we saw were shadowy Russian subs floating ominously beneath us like giant metallic sharks.

After fighting Mother Nature for weeks on end, our mission was complete, and we limped back to Portland, Maine, from Ocean Station Charlie. As we could just about smell the boiling lobsters on the mainland, the Coast Guard received an SOS from a distressed vessel. All other ships were on patrol at various stations, and since we were in transit, heading back to port, we had to respond. Lucky us. We turned back, headfirst into the violent storm we had just narrowly escaped to try and save these civilians. I'll never forget the next morning as we were closing in on the wreck. The seas were turbulent, and the sun had just peeked out of the clouds for one of its rare appearances. We hadn't caught a glimpse of the distressed ship yet, but some of their lifeboats floated eerily by. We stopped to pull them out of the water, hoping to find signs of life. They were empty. Some of the seamen had panicked and tried to escape. They were no match for the merciless crash of the building-sized waves. I sadly imagined their limp bodies sinking down to the sea floor. You can watch a tragedy unfold in a movie from the comfort of a leather armchair but living through the dark reality up close and personal brought the severity of the situation home.

Through the pouring rain we finally got a visual of the ship and confirmed a crew of approximately twenty men and a reportedly drunk captain in need. It was a mess. The crew's largest mistake was made on the docks prior to their departure. The men had loaded their grain onto the ship incorrectly. In the turbulence of the raging storm, it had shifted disproportionally to one side. Eventually the opposite side of the ship, with the fuel tanks, was hoisted into the air. Without being able to draw any fuel, the crew were sitting ducks in a liquid blender of a storm. The crisis was only getting worse as their ship continued to take on water at an alarming rate.

There was a Norwegian vessel already on the scene working to free the men as our military crew approached. The Norwegians were able to successfully extract a handful of sailors by shooting a line across their bow and dragging the men through the churning water. Once we sailed in, the civilians pulled back since saving lives was our job. We initially attempted to deploy a rubber dingy for one big haul. Before it even came close to the wreck, the sea thrashed it around as if it was a Happy Meal toy. We were running out of time. There was no need to reinvent the wheel, so we yanked the rubber boat back in and copied the Norwegians' maneuver. The endangered sailors strapped on double life preservers and tied a rope securely around themselves. They had to take the deepest breath of their life as we dragged them five at a time through the freezing ocean to safety. Icicles were forming on their earlobes. The captain came last and was alone. As our sailors reeled him onto the deck of our ship his skin was purple. The captain's body was brought directly to me for examination. I confirmed his untimely death. Upon investigation, it was clear that, instead of properly securing a loop around his waist, like his subordinates, he intentionally tied a slip knot around his chest. By the time our sailors pulled him over the railing, his chest had compressed, and he suffocated. We saved as many men as we could and headed back home for the second time with the dead captain in one of our empty freezers. His ship ultimately descended to the ocean floor.

Back at port we were assaulted by a barrage of media personnel. The incident was widely publicized. Many of the large East Coast newspapers published articles on it, and my mother actually found out about the tragedy from a story in the *Kansas City Star*. A month after our safe return, I was flown back to Maine for a ceremony where several Coast Guard officers honored each member of our crew with a medal of valor for our team heroics and decisive action in saving human lives. We saved everyone that we could. The only ones who didn't make it were the crew members who panicked the night before any help arrived and the captain.

I was the only physician on that boat, so when someone got into medical trouble, I was plan A, B, and C. There was no other line of defense. In my prior internship there were a handful of veteran doctors in the building that I could rely on for support. Out in the middle of the ocean, I didn't have any relief. I was still learning, but in retrospect, I wasn't as lost as I initially thought. My experience in emergency call at County Hospital and at St. Joseph prepared me well. During the voyage, the Coast Guard required me to perform a write-up documenting every step I took to treat each sailor. After reading it fifty years later, it dawned on me just how capable I was.

Taking on this type of challenge out in the field, maybe to a lesser degree, is a great responsibility and a golden opportunity to expand your comfort zone. It taught me how to rise to the occasion and derive solutions in adverse situations, which is largely a factor of mirroring the successful actions of others. By copying the Norwegian vessel's successful maneuver for extracting the entrapped sailors, our crew was able to save many lives. In this case, it was a matter of life and death. This experience put me on a steep learning curve. I found more answers out in the trenches than I could've in the safety of a classroom setting.

Challenging situations also have the tendency to push you in new directions. I had come close to dying on the East Coast and desired the fulfillment of a partner to share the rest of my life, and a family, with. This was a turning point. My brother-in-law, Tim, was a Kansas City-based anesthesiologist who, with the help of my sister, set me up on a blind date with a stunning nurse, named Mary Beth, who worked at the same hospital. I took her out several times during the Christmas break of my first year in the U.S. Public Health Service, right before I embarked on the aquatic voyage. After the shipwreck, our entire crew was gifted time off, so I flew back to Kansas City in March with a clear head and asked her to marry me. I understood the limits of my own mortality and felt it was the right opportunity to settle down before my time on Earth expired. Mary Beth flew out to New York City for a couple weeks in June, and we were wed that summer in August. I'll elaborate more on this in Chapter Twelve, but for now we will keep it all business. My experience on the East Coast helped me realize there is more to life than career advancement. This priceless wisdom is what you're set to gain from experiencing new, and challenging, endeavors outside of your comfort zone.

WHAT WOULD YOU DO

Note from the author:

U pon completing his final years of training after the two-year residency with the U.S. Public Health Service, in 1968, Terry received his pathology and microbiology specialty from the Mayo Clinic School of Graduate Medical Education in Rochester, Minnesota. His professional career took off as an associate consultant. By the end of his rookie year, he was brought on staff at the Mayo Clinic as a full-time consultant in the Microbiology and Immunology division. In layman's terms, as Google is to the tech industry, the Mayo Clinic is to healthcare. Although this was one of the most prestigious jobs one could land as a young medical professional, the more Terry settled into his new role, the more uncertain he felt about his future.

Dr. Terrence Dolan: During my training, there were lots of organizational changes going on at the Mayo Clinic. Initially, I didn't understand the politics behind them. As a new hire in any big company, it takes time to understand all the things that go on from the standpoint of politics. After spending a few years as full-time staff, I had my ear to what was happening. It was a crucial education. This wasn't unique to the Mayo Clinic; all the big organizations operated this way. It was difficult to do anything new because implementation would take forever. Once I recognized this system would jeopardize the goals I had, I started researching alternative opportunities that would better fit my creative personality.

Although the politics were frustrating, they were the same everywhere. It was just a matter of a different set of players playing the same basic ball game. I've had to grapple with that my entire career. What pushed me over the edge to seriously consider leaving what would've been considered the dream job of most young professionals in the industry was an internal conflict I couldn't rationalize any longer. The Mayo Clinic's philosophy is to have doctors that are hyperspecialized, which allows us to become world-class experts in a narrow area of medicine quickly. I spent five years as a full-time staff member in Microbiology and Immunology, and I became extremely skilled at my craft. I had my own fully-funded research lab, was involved clinically in all kinds of projects, and because I was so proficient in the subject, I started receiving invitations to speak all around the country. Whenever I participated in an event, although I would have slides for the audience to follow along, I'd immediately step down from the podium and stroll through the seated crowd while I presented. This was unusual, but I knew the material from memory and wanted to make it engaging for the audience. As I became a well-known name in the field of microbiology, the requests kept piling up. After giving the same talk to multiple different groups, it became a monotonous routine. I just got tired of hearing my own voice. The Mayo Clinic did extremely well by me, but I needed a different challenge. I couldn't resist the thrill of taking a risk to create something big.

Some people are energized by fame. It didn't turn me on. Although I was grateful to be treated so well, I started to get distracted from why I got into the field. Fame was never a compelling reason. Dr. James Watson Kernohan was a world-famous senior neural pathologist, or brain pathologist, who worked at the Mayo Clinic while I was there. One day while I was walking down the hallway with a group of starry-eyed residents, Dr. Kernohan strode past us in the opposite direction. I gave him a warm smile and said, "Good morning, Dr. Kernohan." Once he was out of hearing distance, I turned to the residents and asked, "Do you know who that was?" They answered with blank stares. I asked another rhetorical question, "Do you recall your educational studies of neural pathology where you learned about the types, descriptions, and basic procedures to deal with various tumors?" They nodded quietly. I continued, "He wrote the book." In that moment it hit me that once you're off the main stage you are all but forgotten. I realized that I *was* on the main stage, getting to be known by the most prominent players in the space, but as soon as I exited stage left, it would transform into, "Who was he again?" Fame is fleeting, and no amount of it was going to give me the feeling of success I was searching for. I had to innovate something that would outlive my name. That's when leaving the Mayo Clinic became a serious consideration.

To be clear, I was still attracted to pathology, but I wanted greater creative flexibility. I could already see that in big organizations you had far less of it. My mentor at the time was a talented physician named Dr. Lyle Weed, M.D.-Ph.D., and chairman of the Mayo Clinic Microbiology Department. We used to eat lunch together every other week. Over one of our lighthearted meals, I told him that I trusted him and confidentially revealed that I was on the fence about leaving the organization. Walking away from such a behemoth company in any industry is a difficult decision to make. It can cause you to frantically second guess yourself. Once you leave the safety of a cushy job to take a chance outside the bubble, you're faced with the unknown. That's a scary foe. Dr. Weed had spent almost his entire career at the Mayo Clinic, so I asked him straight up, "If you were in my shoes, would you stay here for the entirety of your career?" He sat back in his chair and looked at me with a frown of concern. He responded, "I'd do it all over again, and you should too." Well, that's what I expected him to say, and then I'd have just stayed put indefinitely. His actual response was, "No. You have a different vision; you're a risk taker, and you need to move on." Totally caught off guard, I blurted out, "Why did you say that?" He explained, "You're too creative. You've got a lot of good ideas, but you can't challenge an organization as large as the Mayo Clinic, so you're going to have a lot of difficulty capitalizing on them if you don't branch off on your own." I needed confirmation from someone I deeply trusted that had more experience than I did. That said, many of my colleagues stayed at the Mayo Clinic career long and did exceptionally well for themselves. It truly is a world-class organization. I just didn't fit the mold.

Shortly after the one-on-one with my mentor, a new opportunity presented itself. In my off hours, while on staff at the Mayo Clinic,

I taught classes through the American Society of Clinical Pathology and became familiar with a physician who was also putting in a lot of hours there. Before I decided to resign, he mentioned to me, "I've heard of this group in Kansas City that's just starting to grow, and they're small but stacked with talent." This physician made the introduction, and I subsequently got an offer to become a partner. Shaking up my career path was more of an instinctual move than one driven by a clear understanding of what in the hell I was doing back then, but I had a desire for a different kind of challenge. This opportunity fit my criteria to the T. I didn't even look at any other jobs in the area before packing up my microscope within the year.

Change will always be met with resistance. If not internally, then from those around you. It's to be expected, but managing it isn't so easy. Before I formally resigned, the Chairman of Thoracic Disease and several other Mayo Clinic board members tried to talk me out of my decision. I didn't realize the team thought so highly of me. I was both surprised and impressed by their attempts to keep me, even though it made the move even harder to handle emotionally. However, what concerned me even more than the board were my wife's mixed emotions about the situation. She had developed close relationships with the other young doctor wives and considered Rochester home. It was a big comprise on her part to uproot, but she realized that we were relocating closer to both of our families in Kansas City, and that I needed her close support. Last week I read over my original letter of resignation and chuckled, wondering how in the hell I developed the guts to do what I did. I still don't know exactly what drove me to. I just couldn't shake the unrelenting urge to go out and test myself in the real world. In my later years, when the Mayo Clinic honored me with their most exclusive Distinguished Alumni Award, I figured I didn't do too badly. My life plan was incomplete at the time I made this career move, but I drew on the experts around me and took action despite uncertainty.

COWBOY DAYS

Note from the author:

T erry joined a private pathology group in North Kansas City, as the fourth and final partner, contributing his last initial to the name MAWD Pathology Group. During the first decade, the group focused on providing hospital services to the Kansas City region, but at the urging of the hospitals they worked with, the group started a reference laboratory. An information system was then needed to store and integrate all the laboratory's testing data with their various hospital clients.

Dr. Terrence Dolan: In the early 1970s, medical labs had hardly any software to store records and send patient information electronically. One of our partners, Dr. Earl Wright, set out to create a proprietary technology. When I joined the group, I became fascinated with it, and immersed myself in the project. Dr. Wright taught me the basics, and I helped bring it to fruition in analytics and big data. We both lacked any official training in computer programming, so we laid out the design but had to rely on the help of a third-party programmer to perform the technical coding work.

Back then, mainframe computers were the only kind of hardware available. At MAWD Pathology Group, we created the first information technology software to run on one. However, we assumed tremendous risk because, although the programming was documented, it wasn't remotely as detailed as it would be today, which was a big mistake. You have to have a complete record of the underlying coding of any new program so that anyone who didn't originally write it can see the detail of the system in order to make necessary updates and remain in compliance. We didn't have that.

Additionally, if the software malfunctioned, we only had our single programmer to solve the issue, another big mistake.

One situation just about derailed us. Dr. Wright and I were busy working at a peripheral hospital, on what seemed like an ordinary day, when he got an urgent call from the technician alerting him that our mainframe was simmering and might catch fire. This mainframe was running the software for all our private lab operations, and although we had the information backed up to a disc, the room itself wasn't properly ventilated. The heat was building up. Our entire project and data warehouse could've turned to ashes, so we made the executive decision to shut the whole system down.

Needless to say, we were pushing the envelope for what we could do. The continued accessibility and safety of our patients' medical records had to be guaranteed. As the complexity and scale of our innovation grew, we hired a more experienced consultant, Neal Patterson, to straighten out the mistakes we were making.

Patterson was a former employee of Arthur Anderson, one of the largest Chicago-based accounting firms at the time, who had worked in their information technology division for over a decade. He left the big eight firm to start his own consultancy group. Once it became clear Dr. Wright and I were outstripping our programming capability at MAWD Pathology Group, our accountant at the time introduced us to Patterson. We were Patterson's first customer. As his firm grew more client relationships, two other information technology experts joined him, and together they formed the consulting firm: Patterson Gorup Illig.

As we continued to refine the software in Kansas City, an unexpected opportunity presented itself at St. John Health System in Tulsa. At the time, it was a single tertiary referral center that doubled as a teaching hospital for the University of Oklahoma Medical School. The way a tertiary referral medical center works is that a patient will initially be seen at their local doctor's office. Then, depending on the complexity of the case, they'll be sent to a larger community hospital. However, if that hospital is unable to handle the treatment, the primary or secondary care providers will refer their patient to a place like St. John Medical Center, which offers a level of health care obtained from specialists that have a more sophisticated capability to manage the case. The medical laboratory associated with St. John mainly dealt with inpatient testing, or specimen collected directly from its own members, but it also attempted a small amount of outpatient work, testing specimen from individuals unaffiliated with the Tulsa hospital. The pathology group that previously managed this lab had experienced years of problems trying to grow the outpatient side of the business, and because of their poor execution, they ended up developing more internal consternation amongst the medical and laboratory staff than anything else. The hospital administration eventually got fed up, the old pathology group abandoned ship, and the search began for a new team to fill the void.

The medical director of St. John Health System remembered me from a previous meeting some years back. He reached out to me, as well as a couple of my talented former associates from the Mayo Clinic, after his problems came to a head. The director laid out his ambitious plans to bring in a completely new pathology group that could operate as a private practice. This meant that the hospital system would own the physical lab component including all the associated equipment, but the specialists who were needed to turn the lab around would operate under a separate corporate entity wholly owned by the physicians themselves. The other Mayo Clinic physicians that were approached for this project didn't know how to write a private practice pathology contract. I was the only one who had worked in the private space for years, so I knew the ins and outs. I developed an accretive agreement for all parties, where the independent group of pathologists would joint venture with the health system to develop an efficient outreach testing business and then service the commercial laboratory on their behalf.

Transforming a tertiary hospital lab like the one at St. John, which only serviced its own members, into a commercial lab that would perform tests for non-hospital members as well was a simple model, but one that had never been done to the scale we had in mind. To be fair, our idea was really an avant-garde of a unique model that the Mayo Clinic had already started implementing. They had a large clinical lab in downtown Rochester focused on their own customers, and had also set up two additional hospitals, about a mile apart, with very small rapid response protocol labs to handle the outpatient work. The Mayo Clinic had successfully developed an integrated practice. However, when I worked there, I realized that the conglomerate was too slow to make decisions. That experience taught me how to make our new lab more efficient.

Once I joined the smaller MAWD Pathology Group, and learned how private practice worked in comparison, I realized it was much easier to create change and adapt, but harder to maintain the same degree of efficiency through the technical processes. MAWD opened my eyes to the benefits of having a smaller, private team. I decided to blend my experiences and integrate the testing business in a way that wouldn't just solve St. John's immediate problems, but that would outperform all other existing systems and set a new precedent for the medical industry.

St. John's surgeons usually arrived at the hospital around 5:00 am to make rounds and meet with their patients before starting surgery at 7:00 am. The phlebotomists would have to collect these patients' blood specimen first, so the medical technologists in the lab could test them and have the results back to the surgeons prior to them stepping into the operating room. This would allow a surgeon enough time to determine whether a patient, who was previously operated on, needed a change in care and order it prior to surgery that day. Only after the surgical patients' tests were complete would the medical technologists perform tests ordered by non-surgical physicians, who usually started making rounds on their hospitalized patients later, between 8:00 am and 9:00 am.

In a short period of time, from the early morning until about 11:00 am, the medical laboratory would see a spike in the number of tests ordered that had to be performed, but when the volume plummeted outside of that window, the lab's extremely powerful and expensive instruments weren't being effectively used. Basically, the lab was consistently losing money in the afternoon and nighttime until inpatient testing ramped up again the following morning. I realized that the health system needed to figure out a way to surge testing volume in the off hours to mitigate the fixed cost of its equipment. In other words, it needed to bolster its outpatient testing business. The problem was the lab was already struggling to handle its current volume. We first had to straighten out the lab's internal operations before we could feasibly expand the testing business to increase profitability.

Before I came into the picture, the lab at St. John wasn't collecting specimen early enough which caused a chain reaction of bottlenecks in the testing and reporting part of the process. These delays subsequently backed up and frustrated all the non-surgical physician staff members who needed to make their rounds. After I took control, I reorganized the schedule so the surgical patients' blood samples would be collected much earlier, around 2:00 am. We still had to get the surgical patients' test results out first, prior to the start of their surgeries, but the head start would prevent test orders from piling up all at once. After we changed the specimen collection schedule, the complaints stopped coming in, everyone started working together, and we moved on to our next strategic goal.

Private doctors' offices usually didn't open until 9:00 am, so I figured that by capturing their patients' specimen too, the lab would receive an inflow of orders throughout the late morning and early evening. As a result, our instruments would be utilized more effectively all day long. This would generate positive cash flow for the health system and make the business far more profitable, even though it would require additional medical technologists to staff the evening shifts.

St. John Health System was deeply motivated to secure a new pathology group that could get the new lab up and running at full capacity, which is why they gave me free reign to negotiate such an attractive agreement. It turned out to be the deal of a lifetime; however, I had to agree to a verbal contract with my wife that I wouldn't force our family to leave the Kansas City area. I emphasized to the other pathologists, "You've got a golden opportunity here, and if I hadn't made a previous commitment to my wife, I would be seizing it, because this truly is one in a million." I was happy to help them out, as it was an interesting deal to structure. I even coordinated the date for the doctors to move down and start, but when the time came, they got cold feet, and cold feet don't walk very fast.

It eventually became clear to the St. John leadership team that I was having trouble getting the other three physicians to punch their ticket. The board felt blindsided by these last-minute complications and found themselves between a rock and a hard place. They pleaded, "This contract is something we feel will satisfy our needs, and it's something you negotiated so it needs to happen. Will you spearhead this operation?" A German nun turned out to be the unforeseen curveball thrown into my plan of respectfully answering, "No thanks." Her name was Sister Therese Gottschalk, and she was the CEO of St. John Health System. She was a phenomenal woman who grew up on a nameless farm in Germany with thirteen siblings, at a time when the country was still recovering from World War II. Sister Therese was a tremendous leader who joined the Catholic order at twenty-one years old and managed to keep her enormous family out of harm's way during some dangerous times. She had a magic about her when it came to influencing others.

My initial understanding was that I was negotiating a contract on behalf of the other physicians, but after I started working closely with Sister Therese, it became clear she had wanted me to join them all along. Once I revealed that the other doctors had officially turned down the offer, I was the last man standing. She looked into my eyes intently and without a millisecond of hesitation announced, "I hope *you're* coming." I told her I was still under contract with my wife. She shot back, "Why don't you both come visit just one last time then? If nothing else, it'll give us a chance to thank you for the effort you put in. It's the least we can do." This was the fourth and final trip I was planning to take. Mary Beth is the religious one of our pair, so when she found out Sister Therese had the entire worldwide order praying we'd make the move, it changed everything. Checkmate. My wife pulled me aside and passionately confided, "The health system really needs you. We're being called to do this." Called or not, I was eager to seize the opportunity, but I was firm on honoring the promise I'd made to her. Mary Beth recognized there were greater powers at work beyond the two of us, so she made the executive decision to move to Tulsa. With a grin I said, "Say no more."

Sister Therese was an amazing human being. She just passed away, but I'm grateful to have been exposed to a leader with her qualities. After working closely with her, it became clear that whenever I was summoned to her office to "talk", I was going to be helping her with some special task she needed to cross off her agenda. Once I finally realized that, I saved us both time by opening with, "Hello, Sister, what can I do for you?" She would've influenced you too, it was her way. Be that as is may, I now had to follow through on my end of this ambitious laboratory concept. I couldn't let Sister Therese, or St. John Health System, down.

In February of 1980, I made the Tulsa hospital my home base as the Director of Pathology Laboratories. Although I had formally separated from MAWD Pathology Group by this point, I continued to fly back to Kansas City to help them maintain their pace while they recruited my replacement. Every other Thursday I would travel to the "Show-Me State" and work with MAWD all day Friday until their new pathologist showed up. It was a friendly separation. We went the extra mile to help each other through a seamless transition. I've found that burning bridges has one of the most detrimental effects on your career. You never know when you'll need that bridge in the future.

For the first three months of my new role at St. John Health System, I worked twelve-to- fifteen hour days and slept through lonely nights in a modest ground floor apartment on the hospital campus with twenty female nuns in the tower above me. It was hard to relocate alone, but I was deeply confident in, and borderline obsessed with, the success of the task at hand. Mary Beth hadn't been thrilled to uproot from our Rochester home some years back, and it was another big sacrifice for her to pack her life up again. This move was much more complicated. At that time, we had three kids and a 120-acre farm in Smithville with fifty head of cattle and thirty Morgan horses. Even after selling thirty acres of our farm along with all the cattle, it took an army of moving vans to bring the remaining livestock, farm equipment, and household items, plus a flatbed to move the tractors. It was an exhausting process that took a toll on all of us, but this was our best shot at creating something that would positively transform the health system forever. There was no turning back.

When I talk about the "Cowboy Days", I'm referring to the period of my life where my mentality was, "Just give it to me, I'll take it on." I didn't act foolishly, but if I wanted to do something, I didn't really care how dismal the outlook was or what the limitations stacked against me were. It was going to happen. I'm a second-generation Irish American, and that's a common ingredient I've found in all immigrants. My grandparents were poorly educated. In fact, one of my grandfathers couldn't even read or write when he immigrated to the United States. The Irish and English were at war for decades, so to subdue the Irish people, among other things, the English stifled all Irish education.

My ancestors had been deprived of the most basic human liberties for so many years that when they finally had the opportunity to journey 4,000 miles to a country that would offer them the freedom to make something of themselves, they did whatever it took to succeed, as if their very survival depended on it, and it did. This hard-working persistent mentality that was passed down through my lineage blossomed out of immense pressure and deep-rooted pain. It has since forced every generation in my family tree to give their absolute maximum effort in everything they do.

I use Cowboy Days as a label to describe the times, like my move to Tulsa, where I took on a tremendous amount of risk like my ancestors did. However, unlike their hectic experience, although I still had to work my ass off, I was afforded the time and resources to do my homework ahead of time. I knew my downside potential and had detailed plans with contingencies built in to mitigate potential problems that could arise prior to making any life-changing moves.

TRAILBLAZER

I was short-staffed when I arrived in Tulsa. The only remnants of the previous group were two experienced pathologists and two rookies who were fresh out of residency. I clearly didn't have the A-Team, or much in the way of any team at all in proportion to the magnitude of our project, so my first priority was to recruit another veteran leader to help lift us off the ground. Earlier in my career at the Mayo Clinic, I met a sharp Canadian doctor named Dr. John Minielly. He left around the same time I did and ended up joining the McMaster Medical School faculty in Ontario, Canada. Once I signed the contract with St. John Health System, I gave him a call. It proved to be too big of an ask for the previous Mayo Clinic physicians to move one state to another, so you'd think asking Dr. Minielly to move one country to another would've been a slap in the face. After I brought him up to speed on the details of the project, the line went silent. With sincere curiosity, he asked, "Where is Tulsa?" Dr. Minielly came from a family of risktakers. His brother spent three years travelling the world a week after his college graduation, and his son later followed suit with a two-year worldwide sabbatical of his own. Over the years, Dr. Minielly has also taken off for a couple weeks at a time to join his three siblings on trips that have spanned the remote sands of the Middle East to the dense jungles of South America. It was a complicated task convincing him and his family to leave their safe income streams, to move to a new geographic location, and help build a new lab from the ground up, but then again, they have been known to do things different than the average. Dr. Minielly's commitment was the last piece of the puzzle I needed to transform this pipe dream into a reality.

It's difficult to lure talent without a glossy benefits plan or an extensive track record. Without the resources to match the offers of competing employers, all you can do is entice people with your vision for an exciting project. In other words, your edge is being able to clearly map the direction the ship is moving. You had better come up with a compelling pitch, because without allies, your chances of winning the battle with an army of one are low. Fortunately, Dr. Minielly and I articulated our plan well enough to attract some capable pathologists with strong track records. We did eventually hire some promising rookies as well, but only after assembling a core group with experience to drive the strategy. Without that foundation of experience, the structure would've crumbled.

In 1980, we formed an independent professional corporation called Pathology Laboratory Associates (PLA). In 1981, we co-founded Regional Medical Laboratory (RML) on behalf of St. John Health System. Although RML and PLA roll up to different ownership groups, they complement each other for the betterment of the community. RML is a for-profit corporation, wholly owned by a subsidiary of the St. John Health System. PLA, on the other hand, is a pathologist-owned medical group, wholly owned and managed by physician partners. Today there's about twenty-four partners in total. We organized PLA as a separate entity so the interests of our people would be protected. This structure has preserved our autonomy and freedom.

WATERFALL

With a fresh group of pathologists and control over the laboratory, Dr. Minielly and I were ready to start implementing our two-pronged strategy. The first, which addressed profitability, was to increase outpatient testing volume so we would receive new specimen from independent doctors' offices from late morning through early evening. This would allow us to maximize our equipment's capacity with a rigorous twenty-four seven testing schedule. The second prong, which addressed operational efficiency, was to create a brand-new Laboratory Information System (LIS) to facilitate the lab's high-speed operations.

An LIS is a software-based solution that electronically manages each patients' order, mainly recording performance results and current processing timeframes, from when a lab first receives the order to completion of each test. The LIS communicates electronically with a patient's hospital and doctor's office, where it sends the results to directly. I knew that transforming the small tertiary lab into a large commercial powerhouse was a realistic possibility, and fortunately, with PLA, we had assembled enough manpower to start the process. Unfortunately, the success of the lab was still contingent upon the state-of-the-art LIS to manage all the data, which didn't yet exist.

As we started to ramp up our testing volume, I brainstormed with Neal Patterson. Previously, while I was at MAWD Pathology Group in North Kansas City, he had helped Dr. Wright and I create a unique LIS to work on IBM mainframes, but since it was our first attempt at designing a robust program, we made a lot of mistakes. Additionally, minicomputers were coming out, and as far as complexity, they were much easier to deal with and one-tenth of the cost. Patterson suggested that we adapt our old software to work in Tulsa. I countered with a more proactive approach to the looming technological advancements. We needed to obtain a completely new program that was compatible with minicomputers, which were emerging over the horizon.

If we had been able to find an existing, comprehensive software that was compatible with minicomputers to drive the strategy, we would've implemented it immediately. Neither of us had the time to start from scratch. I was juggling enough challenges in the day-to-day management of RML. Additionally, we might've been Patterson's first client, but we were no longer his only. Between developing our technology and trying to grow his consultancy with his two other partners, a handful of staff, and several active contracts, he was swamped. We searched the country for a finished product but came back empty-handed. We had to go back to square one and rewrite a completely new program to run on minicomputers.

As co-designer, Patterson took multiple trips to Tulsa, two or three days at a time, working tirelessly with me around the clock. The main challenge with any kind of team-oriented strategic planning exercise is properly communicating exactly what the desired result should look like. Patterson was a skilled listener, and I had a clear vision of how I wanted the software to function within our laboratory structure. I also brought a few of our experienced pathologists and management staff into the discussions to help articulate ideas. Success in any project of this magnitude would require more than the callused hands of one specialist to bear the load. Patterson meticulously documented our team's conversations and then stepped back with his programmers to breathe life into the blueprint. Slowly and steadily, we inched our way toward production.

Just as the finish line was within reach, a frenetic phone call from Patterson knocked the wind out of me. His first four words spiked my heart rate as the blood in my veins thickened with anticipation. "We have a problem." I told him to go on as my molars started to grind together. The line went silent for an awkward few seconds. Just as I was sure he had hung up the phone, he blurted out, "Terry, we are running out of money. To give you perspective, we won't be able to make payroll in two weeks' time." Click. I huddled with my partner, Dr. Minielly, to mull over our options. Our entire lab strategy hinged on the software they were programming, and we had already come so far. They had to survive.

I immediately boarded a plane to Kansas City. Over a tense dinner I sat down with the three partners to assess the damage. I knew that missing payroll would probably kill their consulting company, so I made the decision, with Dr. Minielly's distant support, to write them a sizable six-digit check. The men across the table began shooting me offers for ownership stake in the company. Sitting around negotiating percentages at that point didn't sit well with me given the nature of our diminishing timeline. Our constraints didn't offer us that luxury. I took a deep breath. The room was still with all three men leaning toward me about to fall off the edge of their chairs. I exhaled, "My sole focus is on protecting this vital software. We're very close to getting it right. I trust your team, and you now have the money to continue the task that we set out to complete. We'll sort the rest out later."

We discussed our immediate path forward until the last piece of steak was eaten. I passed on dessert and walked out of the Kansas City restaurant. Dr. Minielly and I bridged the consultancy's financial gap before payday the following week, which allowed them to avoid bankruptcy. After being rightsized, their bank was able to supply them with the additional funding they needed, and the programming continued.

According to the U.S. Bureau of Labor Statistics (BLS), 65 percent of businesses fail within the first ten years. The mortality rate is extremely high. Normally I wouldn't risk a large amount of capital in pressuring circumstances with such low odds of success, but it was my only option. I believed in what the company was working toward, and I was familiar with the captains driving the ship, so I took a calculated risk, trusting the principals to follow through on their end of the deal. With that said, I knew full well what I was getting into. After all, I was pursuing something that hadn't been done before. For your own sanity, always be emotionally and physically ready to lose if you risk.

When you're young, you can afford to bet the farm, so to speak. When you're more senior like I am, it doesn't make sense to bet the farm because it covers too much acreage. However, regardless of your age, if you have the wherewithal to work your way through stressful situations, you will be in a much better position to take on extra risk, within reason. You will lose money at times, but it'll be a valuable experience if you learn from it. If you lose a dollar, gain two dollars' worth of knowledge. I had thousands on the line.

With an experienced team, innovative ideas, and hard work, we finished writing a novel LIS for minicomputers. We secured St. John Health System's signature for the first purchase contract, contingent, of course, on the technology performing as planned. The alpha test refers to the first time a brand-new software program is run, usually on a smaller, more controllable scale. After the kinks are smoothed out, the software is then moved to a larger health system to run what's known as the beta test. Regional Medical Laboratory carried out the alpha, which is the worst position for a lab to be in since it's associated with the highest risk. We didn't have a choice. Ironically, we ended up overdesigning the software. For the first three years, during the implementation phase, the computers at our disposal struggled to handle the program. It required two minicomputers to run, and even then, it was buggy. When it periodically malfunctioned at the lab during the busiest time of day, 10:00 am to 11:00 am, Monday to Friday, we'd have to cease all operations and manually reboot the system to maintain our pulse. Our saving grace was that more powerful computer models were being released every six months, so, gradually, the hardware became more capable of driving our program.

Many people around me thought passing Patterson's group such a heavy check was absurd, and maybe it was, but it was a decision that made me and my partner a lot of money. More importantly, it transformed the future of the medical industry. By 1984, Patterson's consultancy had rebranded as Cerner Corporation and began selling our completed software, Cerner's first product, named Cerner Classic Pathnet. The program started gaining traction in the medical community shortly after it went live and going public was in Patterson's crosshairs. Before doing so, he had to fly down to a little medical office in Tulsa to straighten things out with me.

Patterson's roots were grounded in a Midwest farming and ranching lifestyle, so he embodied the same cowboy mentality that was engrained in my DNA. Although we didn't come from an identical background, we were both straight-shooting businessmen with an appetite for calculated risks. We considered what a fair portion of company stock would look like, and by the end of the discussion, Patterson's signature was on the dotted line. Because Dr. Minielly had fronted an equal portion of the cash, we divided up most of the stock between ourselves. Another pathologist was instrumental in designing the clinical reporting of the software, so we gifted him a generous sum as well. As you achieve success, be fair with the people who helped you get there. The temptation will be high to succumb to greed. That is a major mistake I hope you will avoid at all costs. In the long run, you will accumulate much vaster wealth by sharing the rewards with your team as the wins come. In principle, it's giving to receive.

I had the option to stay on board with the three other founders, but I was more interested in creating a revolutionary lab. I had no desire to spend all my time with Cerner. Staying true to my original dream and believing in the medical value of our laboratory strategy, I walked away from the big technology business. I did integrate the software with our lab operations to launch RML into overdrive.

FLASH FORWARD – CERNER

I n 1986, without any other obstacle in their way, Cerner Corporation released their IPO with about seventy client users and the sole mission of integrating the medical software we created into health systems on a global scale. As soon as Cerner stock hit the NASDAQ, it saw a mild increase in share price, driven by early investor speculation, followed by a slight dip. Once the medical industry got a full taste of the finished product in action and became fully educated on the long-term viability of the company, the stock price began to soar a few years after the company went public. Within four years, Cerner at least doubled its client user base to 250 and never ran into funding issues again.

Although Patterson's financial and organizational problems were becoming all but a distant memory, my headaches continued to swell because I now had stake in both Cerner Corporation and the lab at St. John Health System while leading contract negotiations for the software between the two. It was impossible to act objectively. As crazy as it sounds, I slowly sold off all my shares during the second mild increase in the late 1980s, netting myself about $2.5 million. I could've held onto the stock and achieved an astronomical return. Cerner has since become a Fortune 500 company, and Oracle acquired it for about $28 billion in June 2022. Retaining ownership of both entities would've been self-dealing, however, and that made me uneasy. I would've directly profited while trying to serve the health system, which became a conflict of interest. Over the years, I've learned that a large purse rarely ever solves an ethical issue. Fast forward to today, and RML is still a Cerner shop, meaning a client user, so the conflict would've never gone away on its own.

Over time, Cerner Classic Pathnet was altered and replaced by Millennium, a proprietary program compatible with newer technology. The program I helped design has since been retired, but it was a stepping stone that lived on through Millennium, which contributed to a significant level of growth for Cerner, increasing its revenue from $245 million in 1997 to over $1 billion in 2005.

I've passed up on just as many opportunities as I've taken, one of the largest being the separation from Cerner. If I had kept control, I would've had to move back to Kansas City and spend the bulk of my time in a field I wasn't as passionate about, which would've dissolved my own happiness and hindered Cerner's success. You can make money in a lot of ways, but you've got to live with yourself at the end of the day. I've yet to see anything positive come out of sacrificing your moral code for cash. How you make your money plays a large role in how you feel once you have it. I prefer to live with a clear mind rather than in a cloud of worry over the what-ifs of the past. Although I sacrificed some wealth by closing out my shares, I'm doing quite well. Life is too short to waste stressing over dollar bills. In any pursuit, don't ever let a pile of money guide your decision-making process or dissuade you from chasing after your true passions. Always weigh the intangible benefits that will have a positive impact on your life and on the lives of those around you. These considerations should form the basis of any judgment call you make in your career.

FLASH FORWARD
— RML & PLA

A s I mentioned, St. John Health System started out as a single tertiary teaching hospital for the University of Oklahoma Medical School. Shortly after my arrival, the system expanded to include three more community hospitals in the Tulsa region. The Sister of the Sorrowful Mother Order, a small Catholic group, had managed St. John for over a century. As the hospital system grew, and soon after Sister Therese Gottschalk retired as CEO, it merged with Ascension Healthcare in 2013. Ascension is one of the leading nonprofit Catholic health systems in the U.S., currently operating more than 2,600 sites of care across nineteen states.

Regional Medical Laboratory (RML), which Dr. Minielly and I established for the St. John Health System in Tulsa, and Pathology Laboratory Associates (PLA), the pathologist-owned professional corporation that we simultaneously created to serve the health care needs of the community, complement each other well. As I previously mentioned, there are two main areas of laboratory medicine. Anatomic pathology includes surgical pathology, cytology, and tissue biopsies to diagnose disease in the human body. Clinical pathology, on the other hand, involves diagnosing disease based primarily on the examination of blood samples and other bodily fluids. RML provides the technical component, meaning the equipment, supplies, and technical support, to carry out both kinds of tests. In total, ten million tests were performed at RML last year, before its merger with Labcorp, with 80 percent of that volume coming from patients outside of our health system. We successfully created a large commercial lab that can do it all, detecting anything from COVID to cancer.

PLA, our independent pathology group, has a contract in place to perform the professional services for the medical labs owned by Ascension, meaning the supervision, interpretation, and reporting aspects of the testing business. Of all the test orders that originate from within our health system, about 99 percent are executed by PLA. Although clinical tests are associated with larger price tags, they only make up a small portion of our group's total revenue. We aim to dominate the anatomic space. The accuracy of our histology section has been analyzed over the years, and a recently published article showed that we have one of the highest surgical pathology accuracy rates in the entire country. Currently, our team performs about 180,000 of those tests a year. For scale, Mayo Clinic Rochester, where I was first trained, tests around 130,000 new specimens a year, which does not include the specimens they review from patients referred to the clinic.

In late 2022, Labcorp, one of the leading global life sciences companies in the world, announced that it had purchased the laboratory assets of Ascension laboratories. RML, one of the largest commercial labs owned by Ascension, had dominated the Oklahoma market for many years. The inclusion of the RML asset was a key part of Labcorp's deal. Prior to Labcorp taking over, PLA had the responsibility of managing both the business and medical aspects of the laboratories owned by Ascension. In the early stages of this intricate deal, both Ascension and Labcorp approached me, on behalf of PLA, to work out a solution that would preserve the current standard of patient care and lead to a seamless transition for all parties. After Ascension notified us about their intention to sell their clinical business to Labcorp, we agreed to comply but negotiated to purchase the rights of their anatomic pathology business. The associated laboratory equipment and six acres of real estate, which included the two buildings we were operating out of, were to stay with us. Next, we worked out a five-year deal with Labcorp to help grow their market share in the state. They hired PLA as the primary medical director of their new assets. Additionally, Labcorp signed a ten-year lease for one of the buildings our group had purchased.

The transition officially started six months ago, and it has gone better than anyone could've expected. All of us are working toward the same goal of having things work out well for the patient first, our client, and taking care of the business side after, a recipe for a successful transaction. This is the culmination of my career, and it feels great.

My early vision for the new laboratory strategy and the accompanying information system was forged through many seemingly insignificant experiences, often deeply frustrating ones, throughout my life up to that point. My success evolved out of identifying those aggravating inefficiencies and creating solutions for them. During the most dark and hopeless times, I drew on the experience of the great professionals around me. I also relied on my unrelenting work ethic to persevere through each challenging obstacle. There is no magic in how I got to where I am. I associated with smart people, put in lots of overtime, earned a few lucky breaks, and strengthened areas of myself where others were weak.

It was a gradual journey. I really didn't know what I was getting involved with to tell you the truth. Perhaps if I saw the challenges ahead of me, I wouldn't have started at all. Sometimes ignorance is bliss. You don't always know what you're getting into, but once you're in deep, you work your way out. I just kept climbing. At twenty years old, I didn't have a clue where I'd be when I was thirty, and at age thirty, I couldn't even fathom what my life was going to look like at age forty. I took it all in one day at a time. I jumped around, took some losses, rode some headwinds, but I never stopped moving forward each day. When you seem to lack all of life's answers at once, don't be discouraged. Remain patient, keep sound company, experience all that you can, and I'm confident I'll be seeing your name behind the next big breakthrough.

"HOW WERE YOU ABLE TO SUCCEED IN SO MANY INDUSTRIES OUTSIDE OF MEDICINE?"

My primary profession didn't afford me the time to figure out every single nuance of the other industries on my own. I had to assimilate a lot. My passionate curiosity to learn drew me to different fields, but before entering any of them, I did my research on who the most knowledgeable experts were. Certain individuals impressed me. I made an effort to put myself in front of them first. In addition to your own study regimen, the most valuable thing you can do whenever you enter new terrain is to ask probing questions of the people who have already become successes. This will help you understand the layout through their eyes. It will shorten your learning curve and enable you to accomplish more with less. Any seemingly *new idea* is really just a *mixture of existing strategies* based off the philosophies of other people. All you need to do is tap into the right contacts and put the pieces together.

I never daydreamed about building a company as a kid. I also never shied away from new experiences as I matured. I took a lot of shots as opportunities presented themselves. They manifested in seven companies from oil, information technology, a commercial laboratory, two private medical practices, a private real estate investment company, and a farming business. Fortunately, none of them have ever failed.

THE ROYAL COLLEGE OF PHYSICIANS

The Royal College of Physicians is an elite medical society in Europe. I'm a part of the chapter in Ireland, so it's the Royal College of Physicians of Ireland. This was something I never thought about until a good friend of mine, who was already a member, invited me to join. My background from a medical standpoint was unique, and my grandparents were born in Ireland, so I was ultimately accepted. I've lived in the United States my entire life, however, the society has added other American Irish in past years. I wasn't the first, and most likely will not be the last, addition of this nature. All my American board and sub-board certifications are accepted over there, so this membership allows me to practice medicine in the country if I ever feel compelled to.

Being accepted to the Royal College of Physicians was an unforgettable memory. Although I'm proud of the personal accolade, I'm more satisfied with what I was able to accomplish for my family. As I mentioned, my grandfather couldn't read or write when he came to the United States. Before he eventually learned to write his name, all he could muster for a signature was the letter X. Upon being initiated as a member, I thought to myself with a grin, "Well, Grandpa, we finally made it. *You* had the last laugh!" This experience fell into my lap somewhat unexpectedly, and you will be presented with similar opportunities throughout your career. Say yes to experience because no one can take that away from you once you have it. In the process, you might just discover the answers you've been searching for all along. Sitting around attempting nothing at all is the worst-case scenario, and avoiding an opportunity out of fear is failure without value. Remain flexible to change, and leverage life experience to shape your body and mind. This is the pearl in life's oyster.

DISTINGUISHED ALUMNI AWARD

Note from the author:

Each year, the Mayo Clinic honors a small number of alumni who've made exceptional contributions to the field of medicine, including practice, research, education, and administration. In 2018, Terry was awarded the Mayo Clinic's prestigious "Distinguished Alumni Award", which is one of the highest honors they give to their physicians. Side note: if the following announcement leads you to believe that Terry has slowed down or retired, you are mistaken; he continues to be a pioneer in the space.

Dr. Terrence Dolan: The Mayo Clinic has been crowned the "number one health system in the world" for the last several years. I was blown away after being identified as one of the few "outstanding physicians" nominated to receive this highly esteemed award. I never would've thought I'd qualify. As I mentioned, accolades, for the most part, do very little for me, but honors like this continue to humble me. Ironically, they remind me to focus on the change I want to make in the world instead of the recognition I may receive for doing so. Add value first, and the rest will sort itself out.

The Official Mayo Clinic Announcement:
"2018 Recipient
Mayo Clinic Distinguished Alumni Award
C. Terrence Dolan, M.D.
Trailblazer in realizing the potential of data analytics in patient care and laboratory management.

Dr. Dolan is co-founder and director of Pathology Laboratory Associates at St. John Medical Center in Tulsa, Oklahoma, and has been managing partner since 1980. He also co-founded Regional Medical Laboratory (RML), serving as president and CEO beginning in 1980 and as a member of its board of trustees. He is a clinical professor of pathology at The University of Oklahoma Medical school, and past president of the Oklahoma State Association of Pathologists. He was a board member of the St. John Health System and is a current member of the St. John hospital board and Regional Medical Laboratory board in Tulsa.

Early in his career, Dr. Dolan recognized the need for a laboratory information system to automate the key processes of the clinical laboratory to improve efficiency and patient care. He taught himself the basics of data processing and software programming and set out to design a computer-based laboratory information system.

He developed relationships with three accountants with whom he developed the initial Path Net Laboratory Information System (LIS). Pathnet, within the Cerner corporation, became one of the major LIS programs in the U.S. and many other countries; it's used by more than one third of U.S. hospitals and clinical laboratories around the world. Pathnet was Cerner's first software product, and Dr. Dolan was part owner of Cerner. In this capacity, Dr. Dolan helped introduce automation and computer technology to the laboratory setting.

He was also instrumental in forming Regional Medical Laboratory at St. John Medical center, which became one of the largest hospital-owned laboratories in the country. It has more than 650 employees performing more than ten million clinical tests. Dr. Dolan led RML as the alpha testing platform for the design of Cerner's laboratory information system, which serves the needs of laboratories around the world. RML's income supports the St. John Health System mission of compassionate and quality care for all, including the indigent.

Dr. Dolan also led the development of the Enterprise Data Warehouse, which has become one of the most robust data warehouses in healthcare. It has gone from the initial harvesting of laboratory data to a plethora of health care data from all facets of health care, including medical, financial, and operational information."

PART TWO

BUSINESS STRATEGY & CAREER INSIGHTS

TWO
THE GAME OF LIFE

"Be not afraid of going slowly, be afraid only of standing still." – Chinese Proverb

"Experience is a hard teacher—she gives the test first, and the lessons afterwards." – Vernon Sanders

"Surround yourself with people that are smarter than you, learn from people who have been successful." – Jack Welch

HE WHO LASTS THE RACE WINS

Dr. Terrence Dolan: I often see impatience behind the ambition of young people. They tend to forget that good things take time. Understand that a big win at the end of your career will give you the perspective of a lifetime of effort. That is, the end destination will gain significant meaning through the journey you took to arrive there. Trying to hit a homerun on the first pitch leads to a lot of unnecessary stress and frustration when it doesn't happen immediately. Don't get too carried away in pushing ahead.

Experiencing the challenges along the road to achievement will develop your ability to sustain any degree of future success. Achieving a big win early on can often have a detrimental long-term effect. The National Endowment for Financial Education illustrates just how dramatic this concept is in lottery winners. It explains, "Over the past couple of years, several news organizations have attributed a statistic to the NEFE, stating that 70 percent of lottery winners end up bankrupt in just a few years after receiving a large financial windfall." These lottery winners missed out on the challenging experiences that would've developed their wealth management skills and allowed them to not just keep but grow their earnings effectively. Their shortcut led to the complete loss of their windfall, and probably their sanity, over the following years. You can't skip the process. You have to earn it.

Don't defeat your ultimate purpose by trying to sprint the entire marathon from the first mile. Instead, maintain a steady pace, not too fast or too slow. The key is finding a sustainable healthy balance between pushing ahead in work and slowing down to play, because the individual who *lasts* the race of life wins. Said another way, *consistent* performance wins this race. Slowly build up to your success.

TICKET TO PLAY THE GAME

I view college as a ticket to play the game. A degree gives you credibility. As a rookie in the working class, it will get your foot in the door with both established and startup organizations when you lack valuable experience. College is an environment conducive to building connections, networking with the future players of the economy, and in your post-collegiate years, this education will serve as common ground with the thousands of alumni who studied at the institution before you. Some of these alumni may become your closest allies. College is also one of the greatest teachers in the subjects of social growth, maturity, and managing responsibility. The challenge of surviving life on your own, dealing with the flaws of others, and learning how to patch the gaping holes in your character might just be the greatest value you're set to gain from attending. I don't view college as a perfect option, but rather, I see it as the most accretive one available at this time, compared to the alternatives, for most young people looking to jumpstart their adult careers. The following are some of the main drawbacks and mitigants I've found. Hopefully, they will help you squeeze the most out of your college experience.

Education is meant to be a bargain, and the cost of enrolling in a college institution is high. Online prerecorded Zoom lectures, due to the COVID-19 lockdowns, have made these pricing concerns even more relevant. Remote instruction has been a recent and unexpected drawback, but one that has been uniform across the board. Unfortunately, only after universities reorganize the large, fixed costs on their balance sheet, beyond the short term, can tuition realistically be expected to decrease. This will largely be out of your control.

Additionally, the lackluster professors and PhD candidate teaching assistants, who haven't yet found their own way in the classroom, that are leading many undergraduate classes make the soaring price tag increasingly disproportionate to the value gained. This is a glaring problem. In my educational history, I've had some outstanding teachers who were pivotal in shaping my career, a lot of mediocre ones, and some that were straight boat anchors. At the time, it surprised me that many of my professors didn't have tangible industry experience to supplement the curriculum they were teaching. These poor performers need to have their pay adjusted, or have their role replaced altogether. On the flip side, all the extraordinarily qualified teachers need to be properly rewarded. This is also out of your control. However, what you can do is look up a professor's unbiased reviews from other students online, review their LinkedIn resume, or directly inquire about their background. This research will net you the greatest return on your hefty college investment.

In regard to the curriculum itself, I recommend taking what you learn in college with a grain of salt. Time renders many textbooks obsolete. Be aware that what is being taught now is subject to change down the road. A current article reflects current thinking in the context of the current market. I suggest having a fundamental background in IT insulated by other courses of direct interest to you. At the very least, you should know your way around mainstream technology, with proficiency in the basic tools and programs used in daily business operations, like Microsoft Excel and Word. Light programming is always a plus too.

Finally, I suggest maximizing your time in college by working an on-campus job or in the nearby city. Especially for those who find school to be a breeze, maintain your momentum. As long as it doesn't detract from your education, work is a great idea. What in the hell you do doesn't really make a difference. Not only did my job as a pharmacist allow me to pay off my medical school debt, but working from a young age also taught me the basics of discipline and time management, which prepared me for life outside the classroom. Through the process, I got a taste of what I did and didn't like about the industry I was committing to for the rest of my life.

For now, a college degree carries more weight than a degree from most trade schools. Attending college will set you up to win in the next phase of the game of life, even though it has its drawbacks. Learning is largely dependent on the character of the student. It's what you do with what you learn that counts. In this sense, college truly is what you make of it.

THE AFTERLIFE, OR AFTER-COLLEGE LIFE

Upon graduating college, you will be faced with two big questions; where to live and what to do for a living. Saving money aggressively will put you in the best position regardless of your answers to the above. Here is how I would approach the next phase of the game of life.

In deciding where you want to live, as far as location, the cost of living will affect your daily life and should certainly be considered, but there are other important factors to weigh, such as lifestyle preference and proximity to family. Do your homework ahead of time to minimize the number of disruptive moves after the conclusion of your education. A wise man once told me, "Decide where you want to live and then find the job. Not the other way around."

Living at home is often the cheapest option if that possibility is on the table. It will lighten your expense load and may even provide you with a means of transportation, like a car. Working through undergraduate pharmacy school while living at home helped me pay off almost all my debt after moving away for Creighton University medical school. However, one of the biggest challenges about living at home, that I had to learn the hard way, is being able to adjust to the differing lifestyles so everyone in the house can live reasonably happily together. In the case where it makes sense, I'd recommend living at home at least until you're established with a steady source of income.

Regarding the second question about career choice, which is largely a subjective matter, I suggest taking the time to fully think through the pros and cons of each option on the table. There may be a few different right answers, but getting this one wrong will take the color out of life. Many intangible factors, such as interest, passion, and quality of life, should heavily influence your decision.

It shouldn't just reflect how big the salary is. No amount of money will be enough to keep you doing something that doesn't excite you over a lifetime. What matters most is enjoying what you're doing every day. This is largely a factor of performing meaningful work, in a favorable location, surrounded by sound company. Strong financial compensation may give you lots of *things*, but it won't give you much lasting satisfaction if you have to drag your feet through muck the whole time. Pursue a career that contributes to, or at the very least doesn't detract from, your vitality in the game of life.

As far as a specific company, working with a nationally-recognized one will give you the opportunity to go anywhere. A large organization usually has a higher transaction volume, greater resources to allocate to your development, and a professional training regimen. This was what I experienced in the start of my career at the Mayo Clinic. On the other hand, a smaller boutique or startup company may allow for more internal control, quicker feedback loops, and greater potential for you to be promoted. However, the management team of a small organization may have less time and resources to teach new partners, like you, while treading water themselves to stay afloat. This was what I learned from my time at the private practice MAWD Pathology Group.

Regardless of size, it's imperative you evaluate a company's personnel, specifically the people you will be in direct contact with on a daily basis. Assuming the standard eight-hour workday, you will probably end up spending more time with them than your family or significant other. Think in terms of the knowledge you're set to gain from those around you as opposed to the superficial glamour of the title and benefits package being offered. You have to weigh how much you're set to learn. When you interview your prospective manager, decide if they are just another boss strictly there to clock in and dish out orders or if they see themselves as a true mentor that will train you to be a successful professional in your industry. At this stage of your career what you need most is not the money, as you will have decades to grow wealth. What you lack is experience and knowledge. As you begin your professional career, that is what I suggest you pursue.

MENTEE – THE ART OF LEARNING

As a rookie in the industry, a mentee, establishing a tight relationship with a successful mentor will rapidly accelerate your development. There is no need to reinvent the wheel, just ask someone with experience what makes the wheel turn. Your primary mission is simple, to learn everything you can from your mentor's career. However, it will require diligent networking and a compelling pitch to get yourself in front of the experts.

Pathology isn't a huge industry, so while I was a young specialist at the Mayo Clinic, I joined various national medical groups to make connections. Most of the meetings fell on weekends, so I'd depart work on Friday afternoons and participate in committee work until my return late Sunday nights. I was always on the road but emerged from the Mayo Clinic with an expansive network of senior academic and private contacts. One of these contacts introduced me to MAWD Pathology Group, in Kansas City, the private practice I eventually left the Mayo Clinic for. Success is much less about what you know and how smart you are as it is about who you know, how hard you're willing to work, and your ability to communicate what you want.

It's worthwhile to develop a compelling pitch. If you've spent time creating one, but still face the disheartening pileup of unanswered emails, being stood up in person, or you find yourself in a deeper relationship with an individual's voicemail box, don't take it personally. If an expert is unwilling to share the knowledge they have, you can conclude one of two things: they're either genuinely drowning in their work, or straight up uninterested in others. Better to avoid the latter individuals. That said, even I have at least enough time to respond to a meaningful email, and my workload is like a child, it never stops growing. I believe these conversations pose great benefits to both sides. The mentee receives a free look inside the mind of a high achiever with answers, while the mentor has the opportunity to personally shape the future of their industry and refine their own core philosophy by sharing the insights gained from their experience. Be confident in the value you bring to the table even when your status is lowest man on the totem pole. Never hesitate to reach out to the top players.

Once you do convince a mentor to speak with or visit you, you have the unwritten responsibility to use their time effectively. One way to do this is by researching as much as you can about their life ahead of time, to gain perspective on who they are, so you don't have to waste time covering their public background. Instead, your goal should be to hit on only the most pertinent questions you need answers to. It may be advantageous to step into the meeting with a page full of premeditated questions in order to maintain the momentum of the conversation. This is not unprofessional. On the contrary, this extra preparation will demonstrate your genuine interest in learning, which will motivate the mentor to put more effort into translating their expertise to you. It will also save everyone time.

A great way to start the conversation is inquiring about a mentor's perspective on new and emerging patterns in the industry, wise and naïve decisions they've made, or how they were able to successfully evolve their career over time. One of the most thought-provoking questions to start the conversation with is, "What was the most significant mistake you've made in your career, and how I can avoid a similar fate in the future?" Leverage a mentor's experience to discover what they'd do differently based on past lessons learned. Try to keep your questions open ended, be specific in what you ask about, and then listen intently.

One final note. It's crucial to end every call or meeting appreciating the mentor for sharing their most precious asset with you, their time. In the same words I say to you, reader, *thank you*.

MENTOR – THE ART
OF TEACHING

As a mentor, on the other hand, your role involves sharing the useful knowledge you've learned through your life experience. A mentor is usually the more senior individual, at least from the standpoint of the knowledge or experience they have. Mentorship is passing on relevant advice, based on lessons learned, forward. It's one of the most valuable gifts a veteran can offer a rookie.

A mentor-mentee relationship is mutually beneficial. As the senior, it might initially seem like a waste of your time. Although being a mentor is a deceivingly subtle gift on the surface, like a pebble tossed in a pond, it has a rippling effect. I've had an old employee of mine show up unexpectedly at my hospital office to reveal how some minor comments I had made five years prior helped completely change the course of his life. I had no idea that our conversation had had such a transformative impact. This is a deeply rewarding opportunity for successful individuals.

Mentorship can also be thought of as the art of teaching. My style is to constantly challenge those around me. I witness an unbelievable amount of talent being wasted because people don't make use of their full capability. At the lab, for example, I met with a mid-level manager just last Friday who is uniquely skilled but a guarded individual by nature, a limiting combination. My goal with a mentee like this is to put them through uncomfortable situations that will require them to stretch and learn something new. Mixing a healthy degree of pressure into my team's day forces them to tap into their innate untouched potential. Even if they occasionally succumb to the pressure, through the process of rebounding from their mistakes, they will emerge with a better understanding of where they're lacking in both their character and ability. These experiences will accelerate their personal growth and the growth of the company. Complacency has the opposite effect.

When my people make a mistake, I put it on a billboard. My intention isn't to humiliate, but rather to capture their attention, so that mistakes are recognized and learned from. The sooner you admit to mistakes, the better off everyone will be. The problem lies in our natural human tendency to overlook our own shortcomings. It makes the intuitive practice of identifying and taking lessons away from mistakes extremely difficult to do on our own. Especially so for young people. This is a vital training a mentor can offer.

While I was grinding through my residency with the U.S. Public Health Service, I received my first training on how to transform mistakes from an impressive trailblazer and my personal mentor. Dr. Frank W. Foote, M.D. was an instrumental pioneer in the field of tumor pathology. He grew up a true country boy, hunting and fishing in a small Mississippi town. He never let that side of him fade even after moving to the Big Apple, working his way up to Chairman of Pathology, replacing a decorated physician in his own right, Dr. Fred Stewart, M.D., at Memorial Hospital, and becoming a Professor of Pathology at Cornell University by the end of his career.

While sitting down with Dr. Foote in his Manhattan office, he introduced me to Dr. Stewart, who became another mentor of mine. Dr. Stewart either didn't have a filter or had one but didn't care to use it. I was never really sure when and what in the hell he was going to say. A colorful but friendly man; one of the straightest shooters I've ever met. Dr. Foote recalled one occasion where Dr. Stewart told him to get another pathologist's opinion. Without taking a step, Dr. Foote looked up at him blankly and shot back, "Fred, you don't really care what he thinks, do you?" Dr. Stewart thought about it for a moment and responded, "You're right." They were transparent individuals, giants in their field, and incredible mentors in my early professional development.

In his senior years, Dr. Foote was an extremely captivating consultant speaker for the U.S. Public Health Service's department of pathology. Every month, during those New York conferences, he would share insights from various cases he was involved with, primarily the ones where he had underperformed or personally made a mistake on. As a good doctor, he knew when he had put his foot in his mouth. He made the point to all of us in the audience, "I won't do this again, and you shouldn't do it the first time." Dr. Foote was confident in his ability to teach, never revealing a cocky ego or wearing a facade of unauthenticity. Walking out of the auditorium I learned that sharing insights from past mistakes are among the greatest lessons a mentor can pass on.

We all mess up because, for better or for worse, no one is perfect. Try to avoid deadly mistakes to your health and career but traverse through life radiating confidence. Just be humble enough to recognize when you fall short, have the courage to set things right when you do and no matter what floor of the building your office is on, be willing to share the takeaways with your team.

"WHY DO YOU STILL CHOOSE TO WORK AT YOUR AGE WITH ALL THE SUCCESS YOU'VE ALREADY ACHIEVED?"

f I had any common sense left, I probably wouldn't be doing this. I've planned to retire from Pathology Laboratory Associates for the past fifteen years, but I keep extending the timeline. Does that make me crazy?

It's uncommon to be working on site at age eighty-five, but I believe I'm making a positive contribution to the community and greater world through my work. I enjoy medicine because it's a worthwhile challenge that allows me to improve other people's lives. With the uncertainty of COVID and all the daunting changes going on in healthcare, I'm also choosing to remain on board for the sake of the younger partners in our group. As an old warrior who has been through a few battles, my message to the team with each seemingly new challenge is, "I've probably seen it before. We'll find a way to get through it."

I'm pushing the envelope. At this stage of the game, the risk is high that I'm going to start mentally deteriorating, but I wouldn't stay if I couldn't adequately contribute. I was just telling one of the younger leaders in our medical group, "Keep an eye on me and if I start slipping, just tell me. You have to speak up; you'll be doing all of us a favor." Two or three weeks later he stepped into my office and confessed, "You know, Terry, the pathologists have been whispering about it, and none of us feel that we could say that to your face." Dr. John Minielly, the cofounder of our group, still lives in Tulsa. I stopped to think for a second and then responded, "Just tell John, and he'll pass on the message to me, don't worry about it." There was another senior director that flashed to mind, so, just to be safe, I quickly added, "If John isn't around, go talk to this guy. However, if I tell you the same joke three weeks in a row and expect you to laugh, that should be your red flag to step in immediately." We created a whole chain of command. The main concern I have is making a significant mistake that could hurt the group. I've been fortunate to keep my mind in good shape, and because I still enjoy the challenge of my work, I prefer to stay out in the field.

My advice is to continue to work hard as long as you can instead of conforming to the commonly accepted retirement age. Retirement is when you're physically and mentally incapable of performing the meaningful work you choose to do. If you lose excitement or are downright miserable in your current occupation, pursue a fresh challenge to fill the void. I don't believe the solution is to completely check out by sitting around in a lawn chair at age sixty-five on a humid South Florida beach or at home watching *The Price Is Right* until you pass on. My mind is still sharp because I *use it every day*. Find something to keep you mentally engaged, not mindlessly entertained.

Working as long as I have has also helped my family get a leg up in the future. I believe that it's up to each generation to set the next one up with the opportunity to have an even better life. Knowing that the ones I love are financially secure has been an empowering feeling. To be clear, I haven't been working for this many years just to give my kids a handout so they can sit around. Rather, I do it to set the example of how they too can set their children up for an even better life. They're already in the process of passing the baton to the next generation.

The game of life and work never stops. Whether you mentally check out or lose your awareness, understand that the clock keeps ticking until your last breath. My advice is to be an active player for as long as you can, ideally up to the last second, because what you don't use, you will lose. Ultimately, it's up to you to decide at what point you are comfortable sitting on the sidelines. Just remember, when you do that, the end is near.

THREE
DOUBLE SHOT OF BUSINESS – STRONG & STRAIGHT UP!

"Recently, I was asked if I was going to fire an employee who made a mistake that cost the company $600,000. No, I replied, I just spent $600,000 training him. Why would I want somebody to hire his experience?" – John Watson Sr.

"If the rate of change inside your business is slower than the rate of change outside your business, the end is near." – Jack Welch

"Business opportunities are like buses, there's always another one coming." – Richard Branson

PAY THE PRICE

The surest way to generate hefty business profits is to learn every facet of your trade and pay the price of time in the game. Draw on patience, realizing there is a necessary process. It's about spending the time to absorb valuable knowledge through direct experience, conversations with experts, and reading, so you don't have to fake it. This is how to become more valuable to the market and to transform your knowledge into personal wealth. This simple concept seems to be accumulating dust in an increasingly complex world.

Learn through direct personal experience. Trial and error are incredibly effective teachers, but they can often be the toughest. Stay active in your field, open to facing novel challenges as often as you can. Even though you will make mistakes, over time, if you are nimble enough to adapt your strategy, they can become some of your most important life lessons.

Learn from the successful experience of others. Interact with the individuals who have paved the way in your industry. They have already conquered the obstacles you are going to face. These individuals clearly found solutions. If they don't explicitly share what those are right away, that's okay, just carefully observe how they operate. Watch what the best in the field do. Of course, that still requires you to be out in the field. You've got to roll up your sleeves and get your hands dirty.

Learn by reading, but I suggest being selective and intentional in the content. By and large, I only read nonfiction autobiographies or business applicable material relevant to a current project or venture I'm working on. I seldom read fictional novels for fun. These genres can be invigorating forms of entertainment, however, from a business standpoint, there isn't a whole lot to gain in comparison to what you must give up. With the limited amount of time in a day to quietly immerse yourself in a book, using it to read what you need to so you can better understand an upcoming challenge or passion may have the greatest long-term effect on your life. Leading up to the acquisition of my first commercial real estate property, I drew on virtually every local market and fundamental investment article I could get my hands on. In starting something new, you may not find all the answers you need by reading, but you'll surely gain a foundation of understanding that will shorten your learning curve. Reading will facilitate your critical thinking ability that will allow you to solve future problems faster.

Regardless of the topic, I must trust an author to commit my time to reading their work. They can only earn my trust if they have successful experience doing what I'm planning to do. After I started the pathology group for St. John Health System, and then began the novel challenge of acting as managing director, I learned a lot from a wise man named Jack Welch. He was the longest surviving CEO of General Electric, one of the largest diversified corporations in the world, reigning over the conglomerate for a staggering twenty-plus years. His resume earned my trust. Welch passed away in 2020, but he was a prolific businessman with a PhD in physics who had an amazing track record of turning around companies. I've never met him personally, but I've read a tremendous amount about him. I've frequently used his quotes in my medical presentations to teach others. Welch was famous for creating an educational center at the company, where he spent the bulk of his time teaching rising executives and shaping General Electric's young talent. Insight from his experience helped mold my own management style. Whether you reach out to someone personally for practical advice or read a book to find the answer, just make sure it's backed by someone who has been there and done that. For any new project, there's a blueprint available to get you started, you just need to find it and fill in the details.

There will never be a point and time when you're too old or experienced to learn something new. Take it from someone as ancient as I am. By doing so, you will not only achieve hefty profits throughout your life, you will also *prolong* your life. Keeping your mind sharp will prevent premature deterioration from setting in. When I finished first in my medical school class, I thought I was the smartest person in the room. Looking back, I was often naïve. I realized that the latter part of the word class is ass. At times, I was one. Instead of being a know it all, you should aspire to be a learn it all. You can never learn enough; it's a lifelong pursuit. Talk to the experts, experience, and learn every single day of your life. Don't ever stop. It may not be the most glamourous way to business success, but it is the surest way.

"DO YOU THINK ALL PEOPLE ARE CAPABLE OF ACHIEVING SUCCESS IN MULTIPLE INDUSTRIES, OR IS THAT JUST WISHFUL THINKING?"

Yes, but with a caveat. If you are willing to sacrifice and able to put in the necessary effort, I think you can be successful at whatever your passion is. IQ has something to do with it, but it doesn't have to be high if you're willing to work hard and learn. You can teach yourself a lot, and others can teach you. No one has to be a giant of intellectual capital to be successful. *But* most people don't work hard. That's the limiting dilemma many find themselves in. It's a personal choice.

Early in my career, I didn't think all that through. As I observed other people who had already achieved what I wanted, I naturally learned. I replicated the patterns that I got from watching and listening to not just smart, but successful, people, and then incorporated my own insights into a holistic action plan that I worked hard to implement every single day. Although the internet has improved visibility and communication with many ultra-successful professionals, it has also brought with it a unique drawback. With such widespread access to the social media frenzy, an inherent danger stems from an army of clever marketers, self-acclaimed gurus that have the ability to spread utter lies through pay-per-click schemes. It's a wise move to avoid these individuals at all costs, regardless of how glorious their get-rich-quick gimmicks may seem. You'll want to listen to the people who have gotten results in real life and sustained their success over time. Pragmatists as opposed to theoreticians.

You don't live long enough to reinvent everything yourself. You've got to learn from other people with experience, otherwise you'll just end up frustrated with empty hands. You may not be as successful as they were, but you'll still be in a better spot than you started out. Try to avoid the common tendency of comparing your progress to overnight success stories on the internet, or someone else's blog post. Instead, focus solely on your personal daily growth. In other words, judge your progress based on where you were the day before, instead of where someone else is today. Everyone's trajectory differs. It's like running a race. Don't look at how far away the finish line is; look at how far you've come.

BALANCING ON THE TIGHT ROPE OF RISK & RETURN

Young people usually spend an ample amount of time thinking through the flashy upside benefits of a new investment, changing careers, moving a state away, or breaking off into the virgin territory of starting a business. The problem is young people don't often spend a proportionate amount of time preparing for the sinking curveball. They are subject to not understanding downside risk, which is the likelihood of a scenario taking the most unfavorable turn possible, pushing them far outside of their comfort zone. This is a pitfall to avoid. Figure out what's on the line for you ahead of time and devise a plan to get yourself through the worst-case scenario before you find yourself in quicksand.

Obviously, having a firm understanding of what you'll receive for accepting the downside potential is also vital knowledge to have. It's the payout, reward, or return that justifies assuming any degree of risk. Along with the monetary return, starting a business can also include the intangible upside benefits of creative flexibility, lifestyle balance, and career enjoyment. Always weigh your risk-adjusted return before tiptoeing the line.

If, after thorough investigation, the benefits of a new venture outweigh the downside risks, and it makes sense to journey onward, understand that you will make mistakes. Risk-taking and mistakes are a package deal. Although you do gain invaluable experience through the process of learning from them, the key is to keep yourself in the game, able to fight another day. In other words, realize you're going to make a great deal of mistakes in any new business endeavor, so don't bet the farm. Cap your downside risks so they are manageable. I recommend practicing calculated risk-taking, a strategy that requires thorough research ahead of time on what could go wrong and devising an action plan with built-in contingencies. There will always be something that doesn't quite play out like you thought it would. If you've already prepared yourself for the worst-case scenario, as it's developing, you won't be blindsided or waste time panicking. Most importantly, equipped with actionable plans and a clear head, you'll have a much higher success rate. Get the facts, analyze the data, and then ask questions before taking any opportunity involving risk. Then, be ready to lose, and if you do, go out and make it back. It's the greatest perk of being young.

IS RUNNING A BUSINESS RIGHT FOR YOU

I n starting a business, you have to bear the brunt of risk. Some people just can't stomach the feeling of their hair being on fire. Although I consider myself a risk taker, I don't take on as much risk as it would seem to an outsider since I do my research and think practically through the downside before I step up to the plate and strike out. When I was younger, I struck out faster than I did as I got older. That's called experience. The key lies in not swinging at the same crappy pitch over and over again.

Most people can't start a successful business because they are too risk averse with a crippling fear of the unknown. Most people don't have the wherewithal, or craziness perhaps, to mentally handle risk. However, you don't take on as much if you do your due diligence. Have no doubt about it though, it will still get dicey at times since no deal is guaranteed. When everything is up in the air, you'll have to decide if running a business is right for you.

SIX GUIDING PRINCIPLES: ADVICE FOR THE CRAZY INDIVIDUALS WHO ASPIRE TO RUN A BUSINESS

One. Start your business out of necessity. I've built seven companies that've never failed because they addressed problems that I, or others in my community, needed solved. No one had proposed a viable solution at the time, so it made sense to derive one with a company. My partner and I came to Tulsa to establish a high-powered medical laboratory and pathology group because the health system was beckoning for help with implementing a new business model. I suggest solving a long-term problem in an industry that you have a passion for and can grow in.

Two. Pursue innovative ideas, but don't get spread too thin chasing after different ventures. Identify the idea that makes the most sense, put all your effort into taking that shot, and stay the course as long as it's feasible. If things don't work out, after giving your best effort, cut your losses, move on, and pursue the next idea with lessons learned. As I mentioned before, doing your homework makes this process far less risky. Channel all your focus into the best one or two ideas and follow them using detailed plans, refined by your experience and the experience of those who have already been victorious. If you spread yourself too thin, you will deplete the energy, time, and attention necessary to make any of your business opportunities succeed. You'll end up with a dozen mediocre or failed projects rather than a few masterpieces. The key word is focus.

Three. Expect the unexpected. As an owner, crazy can get crazier because in business you're dealing with humans. As the boss, you have the power to organize your business internally. Leave uncontrollable chaos on the outside. To do this, you must adapt to unexpected situations with a cool head and innovate solutions quickly. The path of starting a business will be riddled with unexpected challenges. Don't let the curveball catch you off guard. Now that you know with full certainty it is going to come, you can prepare yourself to smash it out of the park.

Four. Be careful of flaming out but work like hell. Pace yourself to survive the long-term game. Become a master of managing your stress levels and recognize when you need to take a break to ensure future capability. There will be another day. You need to find your own sustainable work-life balance and have patience while your business grows. Avoid getting caught up in the minutia of the day. Instead, look toward the greater goals that motivate you.

Five. Seek advice from those you trust when starting a company, but don't take it from anyone who hasn't achieved the successful outcome you desire. There is no need to solve a math equation if someone before you has already derived a solution for it. Make connections, ask questions, and then implement the insights you receive. Even at my age, I ask for a second opinion depending on the circumstance. What matters more than the question itself is who you ask it to.

Six. Do something to improve your mind, body, and career every single day. Be aggressive in your development. The key is daily growth. I always worked hard to maintain my business and career momentum, something that has helped me glide through many areas of life. While I was at MAWD Pathology Group, I took it upon myself to learn the basics of software programming, which led to the completion of Cerner's first product and my success with Regional Medical Laboratory. Later in my life, while I was considering an exit for my oil company, I worked overtime to educate myself on commercial real estate. This research allowed me to hit the ground running once I transitioned to the new industry. I accepted the responsibility of controlling my future and took consistent action to accomplish what I set out to do. It's a principle of success; you're either growing or falling behind. There is never standing still or maintaining; that's a figment of the imagination.

"HAVE YOU EVER DONE A BUSINESS DEAL OUTSIDE OF THE U.S.?"

As far as a real estate deal or starting a company, no. I've stayed clear of those because you have to have a deep understanding of each country. They all have their own nuances. The language barrier is a significant challenge to overcome. England and Ireland speak the same language, with some variations, but neither of them speaks Tulsa. That said, I did work out a deal to purchase an unexpected product in the Middle East. There are some things in life you can pass up on. An invitation from the King of Saudi Arabia is *not* one of them.

The College of American Pathologists is a nonprofit professional group comprised of about 18,000 board certified pathologists with a mission of advocating best practices in pathology and inspecting medical laboratories nationwide. Shortly after the organization was established, the U.S. government gave the group accreditation status to confirm international compliance worldwide. I was an active member in the group that only inspected U.S.-based facilities. My colleague, on the other hand, a Virginian doctor named Washington Winn, which we promptly shortened to Wash, was performing critical inspections in some of the most exotic places around the globe.

The first time Dr. Winn was scheduled to go to Saudi Arabia, he called me up to see if I would join him. I declined, as I had tunnel vision for growing my other businesses. On-site inspections occur every two years, so when he asked me to join the survey team for a second time, he reasoned, "These labs are operating on your Cerner software and are struggling to maximize the full capability of the technology." I packed my bags.

Saudi Arabia wasn't very welcoming to U.S. visitors at the time. However, we were on the king's visa, which opened the gates to the kingdom. I had to sign away my American rights to enter, but I held a golden ticket directly from the crown. I never dreamed I'd be in a position to experience this when I was young. My upbringing didn't afford me the same exposure to the world like today. I never even flew on an airplane until I was in my late teens. Now I was flying in first class to the capital of Saudi Arabia. Our jet had a layover in London, where women who emanated wealth boarded the aircraft dressed to the hilt in jewelry and fine clothes. The minute we touched down in Riyadh, they were veiled in all black robes.

My wife opted out of going to Saudi Arabia because she didn't feel comfortable traveling there during the turbulent times. She might've inadvertently gotten me thrown in jail if she had tagged along, and that's not a joke! Across the Middle East, women were viewed as subservient to men. They couldn't even eat at the same dinner table.

One of our lab techs shared with us a foreboding story about an English physician who had worked in Saudi Arabia on contract and decided to bring his wife along. One day, the physician's wife took a short excursion to the local market while he was at the hospital. It was the peak of summer with the golden sun beating down on the arid desert sand. She wore short sleeves, without a hijab, as if she was cruising along the palm-tree-lined coast of Southern California. Only she wasn't. After briefly gathering her groceries, the religious police approached her and ordered her to cease shopping immediately. She didn't have her own car, because women also weren't allowed to drive at the time, but she did have a private chauffeur. The government agents helped her swiftly load up the food and then escorted her back to her residence. Without any explanation, the police then proceeded to the hospital and arrested her husband. They stated that it was his responsibility to control his wife. He had failed to do so, which was a criminal offense. The lab tech's chilling story made it clear that I was no longer in downtown Tulsa.

From the minute our team touched down we were accompanied by military escorts dressed in plain clothes. It was eerie going out at night, as a group of western foreigners. We stuck out like sore thumbs and got many ominous looks from locals. That said, after spending some time in the country, I found Saudis to be extremely welcoming, a pattern I've seen all over the world. People are people no matter where they're from. The majority are good, and a small group are radicalized, which give the rest a bad rap. Travelling is a great way to experience diverse cultures, grow your emotional intelligence, and understand people with different perspectives.

The king took care of us because he wanted a passing evaluation for his medical labs. Their labs had already been inspected more than once before, and they maintained high standards, so they *were* in certifiable condition. A few did run into technological trouble, but we were able to identify their acute issues with the Cerner software, offer solutions to optimize their capability, and then quickly move on to the next facility.

Something that came as a surprise to me was that Saudi Arabians are some of the largest purchasers of Iranian carpets on the planet. I didn't know anything about fine carpets when I got there. Anyone could've pulled the rug over my eyes. Dr. Winn, our team lead, on the other hand, was a connoisseur of Middle Eastern, and Iranian carpets in particular. One night, just as he was about to disappear on his latest search for another fine piece to add to his collection, I offered to keep him company. My motivation stemmed more from boredom than curiosity.

The extremely fine pieces were on the second floor of this enormous warehouse, with several hundred years' worth of carpets all rolled up on their ends. Wash whittled down a triple-digit pile to two, at which point he found himself at a stalemate. They were both gorgeous, even an amateur like me could see that. I chimed in, "Why don't we buy both, and you can decide before we fly back to the U.S. which one you want. I'll take the other." The price tags on these fine pieces were arbitrary. To close the sale, we had to negotiate, and that could only be done over a warm cup of tea. This was a new one for me, but as they say, when in Rome, or Saudi rather.

Upon my return to the American Southwest, I could see the awe in my wife's gaze when I showed her the special souvenir I had brought back. After some research, I lightly mentioned, "If you want more, it won't require an eighteen-hour flight." As you can imagine, the list was short. There were only three sellers of authentic Iranian carpets in Tulsa. Only one had the superior quality I was looking for. I bought about twenty from Amadi, the owner, and we became good friends over the following years. After 9/11 occurred, public prejudice and uncertainty killed his business. He called me up and sighed, "I've got some items I don't normally offer, but times have changed. I need to sell." I visited his shop, but after inspecting the inventory was left unimpressed. He could see my discontent. Without a word, he looked up at me with a slight grin as if he knew exactly what I wanted and led me to the back of his private office.

In my house, a huge carpet spans almost the entire wall in the front room. It was originally owned by the Shah of Iran. When the Iranian people ran him out of the country, a myriad of valuable items from the palace were either lost or promptly sold. Amadi's father was a skilled carpet dealer in the region and snatched it up right when it came available. The carpet is an intricate piece to be hung up and one of only two specially woven for the Shah. This incredible piece of art is still pictured in many Iranian history books, so I'll probably donate it to a museum if I ever part ways with it. I never executed a business deal overseas; however, I did acquire some world-famous carpets and was part of a team that certified the King of Saudi Arabia's hospital laboratories.

"DOCTORS ARE KNOWN FOR BEING NOTORIOUSLY BAD BUSINESSMEN; HOW WERE YOU ABLE TO BREAK THE STIGMA?"

It's true that doctors are usually lousy at business. For the most part, that's a good thing. I personally don't want my doctor to be a good businessman. If that's the case, he's always going to be looking for a return on investment. All I want him to focus on is making me well. My first love has always been medicine; my hobby is business.

Time has been my friend, my greatest asset. Most people's careers span about thirty-five years. At my age, still clocking in full time, I've done that and am probably rounding out what could be considered a second career. I'm a long-term player with more experience than average. Over the years, I learned the art of business by overcoming tough challenges and associating with extraordinary individuals.

I also read a tremendous amount. Medicine is an industry that evolves at light speed. I have to read extensively to stay current on what the hell is going on. I've used this habit to shorten the learning curve of all types of projects I've taken on, including those in business. My line of work got me into the routine of reading a fair amount each day. Although there are some days, like when I'm at the lake house, where I may not do much, I'll always do something.

My parents taught me to learn everything I could as a young boy. I didn't listen very well at first. In grade school I was a terrible student to a point where my poor mother had to sit in on a few of my fourth-grade classes, an embarrassing punishment, to make me realize how far I was slipping. I just wouldn't apply myself. I lacked confidence. Once I realized that hard work could compensate for a lack of brains, I started to claw my way back. My first 100 percent on a grueling math exam in seventh grade was a turning point for me. I developed a passionate curiosity to learn. At that point, it became a worthwhile challenge moving forward, and I got my act together. The trick is I stopped perceiving learning as a painful job. I don't have to force myself to do it. I choose to learn each day because it's enjoyable. What effect could this reorientation have on *your* life?

IS LUCK LUCKY

For the most part, you make your own luck. It's how you live your life and act around others. This is what I call "earned luck". It's being around the right people, at the right time, but it all falls into place because you worked your tail off to get there. I also believe in the presence of "random luck", characteristic of the times when you can't seem to conjure up an explanation for how perfectly the stars aligned. There's no doubt about it, I received some of that too. Appreciate these unpredictable gifts and take advantage when they come. From the mouth of Earl Nightingale, "Luck is what happens when preparedness meets opportunity. A great opportunity will only make the unprepared look ridiculous."

FOUR
YOUR MOST VALUABLE ASSET

"Coming together is a beginning. Keeping together is progress. Working together is success."
– Henry Ford

"A brand for a company is like a reputation for a person. You earn reputation by trying to do hard things well." – Jeff Bezos

"Good management consists of showing average people how to do the work of superior people."
– John D. Rockefeller

LEVERAGE: THE TURBOCHARGER TO A BUSINESS ENGINE

Note from the author:

Don't be the plumber who cleans the toilet, be the owner of the plumbing company counting the checks in the high-rise office. A thorough breakdown of what Terry refers to as "The Law of Leverage", in reference to borrowing other people's money, can be found in Chapter Eleven. This section will only discuss the power of leveraging other people's labor as an effective tool to boost business profits.

Dr. Terrence Dolan: Don't work for the entirety of your career making someone else rich. Working for someone else can be positive when you're just starting your career, but only if you're learning enough to compensate for the hefty time investment. Eventually, your target should be to cross over to the ownership side.

There are various management tools and strategic decisions an owner can make to boost a company's profit margin. Leveraging other people's labor is one of the most effective ways, but only if the benefits are passed on to contributing employees as well. Pay for value, and share the upside. Taking advantage of labor has an extremely counterproductive effect. Put the right incentives in place from the start so that, as the business does well, everyone who contributes does well too. This will allow you to retain the best people. Mediocre labor won't make you rich, talented labor will.

On the other hand, adding employees also increases risk. They can make internal coordination more difficult, complicate communication lines, and add to an organization's liabilities. This is why I disagree with the common advice to scale up quickly. Instead, I suggest starting small and staying small for as long as you can. At some point, however, as your company grows, you will have to hire additional employees to maintain momentum. There is no way around that, but there is also no rush to get there. Hiring new employees brings its own set of unique problems that you'll ultimately have to deal with. A useful rule of thumb is to focus on adding people to payroll only after focusing on the mechanics of the business itself. Make sure the engine is running smoothly before adding passengers to your vehicle.

For a small startup company, I would try to limit the amount of full-time employees on payroll and outsource as much of the work as you can to independent contractors to avoid excess liability and unnecessary complexity. With our commercial real estate investment company, we have one property manager and one accountant on payroll. Our property manager is on the front lines of the business, checking in with tenants, speaking to owners, and maintaining the physical shape of the buildings. Our accountant keeps records of all the business's financial transactions. The remaining duties we handle in house are shared between our two employees, such as finding leads and marketing. All other tasks, like hiring a contractor to fix a broken window or getting legal advice, are outsourced as needed.

Leveraging other people's labor is an effective way to accumulate wealth in the capitalistic structure that our country was founded upon. But, crossing the line and taking advantage of someone else should never be part of your business plan. Understand that money is the justified reward a business owner receives for setting up an organization that allows them and their employees to earn a living in return for offering a valuable product or service to the market. Harness the power of leverage by making a return off other people's labor. This is the turbocharger to a business engine. It adds horsepower.

THE AXE

P eople are your most valuable assets. The success I achieved wasn't just a result of my own capability, it also stemmed from my ability to attract extremely talented people and guide them in the direction I needed them to move. Stay away from the individuals that pull you back. Surround yourself with the ones that are willing to grow with you. This is my secret to business success.

I've never ordered a layoff in my career, and I never will. That said, adverse market impacts, due to something unpredictable like a worldwide pandemic, can throw an organization off pace. It's almost impossible to perfectly anticipate that sort of situation. However, if a company has the discipline to diligently prepare during prosperous times and implement standard protective controls, such as keeping a certain percent of reserves on hand, it will have other options in the event of a sudden downturn. During the COVID-19 pandemic, faced with a 60 percent initial decrease in volume at our lab, we stayed true to our people without firing any lower-level workers or slashing salaries to get by. In fact, new employees joined us. Because we upheld our corporate controls, we were able to fall back on reserves to complete payroll when we found ourselves in a pinch.

Our compensation structure starts with each partner receiving a base salary. Then, depending on how well we do during the review period, excess bonus funds are dispersed, usually starting in May, three times until the end of our fiscal year, which concludes at the end of December. Once COVID hit, we just withheld the bonuses. In the end, it only turned out to be a temporary delay. After a few months, volume came roaring back. Because we had all hands on deck when the market started to recover, we were able to meet the overwhelming demand immediately. Our group performed so well that a new bonus was initiated by August of the same year.

We slowed down but kept everyone in the game. When the market turned, we were able to hit the ground running with a full roster.

The widespread medical layoffs that occurred in the wake of the COVID-19 pandemic came as no surprise to me. Executives at many well-known organizations, like Hertz and GNC, collected millions in bonuses just before filing for bankruptcy. The reason many of these companies had to file in the first place was because their leadership teams had allowed too much debt to accumulate. The pandemic put the mistakes of these over-leveraged organizations on a billboard. When the walls came crashing down, the higher ups cashed in their bonuses by withholding their employees' wages and initiating widespread layoffs. Slapping a Band Aid on a knife wound won't stop the bleeding, you must go to the source of the bleeding and properly address it. This was a case of short-term thinking in a long-term situation. There is a hefty price to pay for that approach to both life and business.

These executives sacrificed their reputation and future success for the lust of a cold dollar. Although their pockets are full for the time being, when the money eventually dries up, and they become desperate for a talented workforce to expand the business, shady actions and a tarnished name will manifest in the type of person that would be willing to return to the same bosses who laid them and their loyal colleagues off.

In the wake of a sudden slowdown, our pathology group's business model is to focus all efforts on growing revenues rather than trimming the organizational tree to cut costs. Instead of laying people off, our main focus will always be geared toward new business development to pay the bills. It's not always cut and dry, as the alarming COVID disruptions did make the situation more complex, but the responsibility of preparing a company to survive downturns and to preserve its workforce falls primarily on management's shoulders. Layoffs are usually failures of management rather than failures of the people being managed.

Employee job hopping is now becoming the norm in our society, a cultural shift that has been so dramatic the movement has even earned its own nickname: "The Great Resignation". Have you ever wondered why employees lack confidence in the companies they work for? According to Willis Towers Watson's 2022 Global Benefits Attitudes Survey, "Forty-four percent of employees are 'job seekers' with over half of those workers stating higher pay was a top reason they'd look for a new job." When layoffs and salary cuts become a common pattern at a company, would you have confidence in it? Many management teams and business owners are so quick to forget how much value one loyal, hardworking employee can contribute to their mission. I hope the pandemic made them remember.

If you recall from Chapter One, the cofounder of our pathology group is Dr. John Minielly. I believe the rapid success of our company has primarily been a factor of us being able to retain our talented personnel. One of the most important lessons I've learned about retaining talent is that you must treat your people fairly from a financial standpoint. Even though Dr. Minielly and I were the founding members of the group, we split up the shares of ownership in the business evenly amongst our original team, although I did retain the voting shares in order to keep us moving forward in the event of a prolonged standstill, which I've never had to use. Our partners understood we had no financial ulterior motives, which cleared the air of doubt and facilitated a mutual trust that has kept them cooperating with us in the long term. A successful business compensates in proportion to the value it receives. This precedent is why our company continues to achieve new milestones.

In 2020, compared to previous years, our industry saw about a 20 percent reduction in new pathologists joining the workforce. That same year, our lab experienced a 40 percent increase in testing volume. Because we kept our best people, business is booming, even as the supply of our vital specialists steadily decreases. When I was a rookie, I didn't realize how much one strong ally could really contribute to an organization's goals. I gradually learned the power of this truth as I gained more senior experience. Treating your people right pays off big time. Don't be the axe that stifles improvement, become the water that helps everything blossom around you. A rising tide lifts all boats.

REPUTATION: INVISIBLE GOLD

R eputation is how to stand out in today's business world. Like invisible gold, it isn't tangible, but it carries immense value. Reputation is the key to attracting top-tier talent, cultivating long-term relationships, and bolstering your organization's profit margin.

People are at the heart of any company. One of the most effective recruitment tools is developing a positive reputation in the industry. This is often a matter of treating others well. I remember a unique situation where one of my young pathologists was dead set on leaving our team because his wife couldn't stand the slower Tulsa lifestyle. After trying my best to talk him into staying with us, it came to a point where I had to respect the decision he was making on behalf of his family. I then switched to the how-can-I-help as opposed to the screw-you mindset and wrote referrals to every health system he asked me to. I may have lost a bright young pathologist that day, but because of how I handled the situation, I will likely gain two more in the future. Treating others correctly over my career built me a credible reputation that allowed me to gain the trust of others. This attracted the best professionals in the field to our pathology group, and they were a tremendous influence on our rise to the top. This is a part of my philosophy I will never deviate from.

A positive reputation will speak volumes to potential partners about how they can expect to be treated. It will allow them to set expectations about what their experience will be like with you, even before you have a chance to pitch your case. More often than not, these individuals will share the conclusions they draw with their friends. Hire one outstanding employee while maintaining a strong reputation, and pretty soon you'll have three of their peers lining up for an interview. Although it takes time and experience to earn a reputation that tells a positive story, it's imperative to leverage the power of referrals. On the flip side, no one wants to deal with a shady past. This kind of news spreads even faster in our society, driven by electronic internet sharing. It'll leave you fighting tooth and nail for the bottom of the barrel.

A powerful reputation isn't just the best way to recruit top performers, it's also the key to keeping them after they join. Without a feeling of trust there is no relationship. You've got to understand your business through and through, so you know what you're talking about. Become knowledgeable so you can tell the truth. In the words of Warren Buffett, "It takes twenty years to build a reputation and five minutes to ruin it." A single lie can destroy your whole reputation. As a business leader with a firm knowledge base of your field, clearly lay out the strengths and weaknesses of each project you're involved with and be open and willing to search for clarity on things you aren't sure about. Over time you'll build trust amongst those around you. Your people will stay with you because of it. This is one of the best ways to retain top talent, the heart of your company, and they'll build your business.

The actions that built my own reputation were driven by the belief that if everyone does well, I win. I started my career chasing personal accolades. As I gained more experience in dealing with people, both professionally and otherwise, I witnessed the detrimental cost that expedience has on long-term relationships and career success. My tactics matured. I reoriented myself to the collective. I've been astounded by the number of individuals I've gotten to know through my business dealings who later reached out to me for medical advice. These business professionals saw how I played their game, with fairness and transparency, in a field that they were familiar with. Next thing I knew, when they or their family had a medical complication, my cell phone would light up. This dynamic has awakened me to the status of my current reputation and all the advantages it has brought me, including my first few deals in commercial real estate, which I will explain in Chapter Nine.

A solid reputation can also speed up business transactions. My real estate company deals with brokers daily. They no longer make our team sign compensation agreements before connecting us with tenants looking to rent our retail space. These brokers trust us and know we will always pass back a check if we end up leasing to a company they represented. Our reputation has accelerated the process of filling up our buildings, which has kept the cash flowing into our business.

Finally, a favorable reputation will drive up your profit margin. One of my former medical friends, patriarch of his household, sadly passed away at ninety-five. This man's family needed to free up some money to fund his funeral, so they decided to sell one of the properties in his portfolio. Over the years, they saw how I conducted myself as a friend to their father, as well as a professional in both the medical and real estate space. They trusted that I could close quickly, so they sold me the property at a reduced price. It worked out well for all of us. A good reputation pays, literally.

Sam Walton, the founder of Walmart, and one of the world's richest people during his life, was revered by the public throughout his time leading the company. He exemplified how to treat others. During the latter part of his career, Walton and one of his canine companions, Ol' Roy, would travel nonstop, from Walmart to Walmart nationwide, to personally meet with and motivate Walmart's employees on the front lines. Walton stayed humble, never putting himself above the job or the individuals working under him. In his own words, "I learned a long time ago that exercising your ego in public is definitely not the way to build an effective organization." It turns out he knew what he was talking about.

Walmart was founded upon the foundations of value and affordability. In congruence with this philosophy, Walton used to take a red Ford F-150 on his hunting trips with his two dogs in the truck bed. When the billionaire was asked about the old truck by a nosy reporter, he famously shot back, "What am I supposed to haul my dogs around in, a Rolls-Royce?" The dents and scratches that it accumulated became a symbol of his reliable and hardworking nature. He was a business leader that always stayed true to who he was and the beliefs he held dear. Does it surprise you that during his tenure the company grew exponentially, backed by an army of staunch employees? Just as Walton reaped the lucrative benefits of his reputation, so can you.

FIVE TIPS ON MANAGING HOMO SAPIENS – AN IRRATIONAL SPECIES

One. Understand that managers are paid to deal with challenges; it *is* the job description. Whether you're managing ten or one hundred people, anticipate they won't follow through. The question is, how will you respond? Take a progressive approach to move forward when human nature is to respond angrily. Be objective, able to stomach failure, losses, people, and proposals without overbearing emotions so you will have a clear head to make decisions. Successfully leading a team is often a balance between managing others and managing yourself. Be the solution to tough situations instead of contributing to the problem.

Two. Practice tell-it-like-it-is management. Say what you mean and mean what you say. To make this easier on myself, I keep my professional relationships distinct from my social relationships. I'm friendly in both cases, but my employees aren't necessarily the same people I'll grab a beer with on Saturday night. Social relationships are important—no one would be happy without them—but I maintain a healthy separation. Of course, I still admire the people I work with. I've just found it easier to manage, from a business standpoint, by not blurring the lines. If I'm dealing with business, I leave the rest alone, which makes the tough decisions less stressful to communicate. Mixing social and business hours can add unnecessary complication to your life. As a manager, you must be prepared to say "no", which is a much harder response to a friend than a business associate. Although your delivery will vary from person to person depending on their personality, your underlying message should remain the same. Tell it like it is.

Three. Only work with an individual that has a comparable or better reputation than your own. As George Washington famously said, "Associate with men of good quality if you esteem your own reputation; for it is better to be alone than in bad company." Of course, that implies developing a strong reputation for yourself. Become a careful thinker in business interactions. If you don't know something, it's much better to respond, "I'm not sure about that, but I will do my research and follow up with an answer by x date or time", rather than lying your way around what you don't know. Even as a manager, you don't have to have all the answers as long as you're honest and stick to your word to try and find them. This approach will build you a favorable reputation that will attract others of similar quality. It will establish a cooperative work environment, credibility with your team, and mutual respect. To effectively manage anyone, you will need these key ingredients.

Four. Focus on improvement *and* on things done well. As mangers, we often fixate on our teams' weak points, usually highlighting a small percent of mistakes. Don't let innovative thinking go unnoticed. It is foolish to disregard the human need for recognition. For every shortfall your team has, there will likely have been double the number of successes. Recognition will motivate your team to keep pushing forward and help prevent burnout. Effective management requires perspective, which means giving credit where credit is due. Share the wins with your team and more will come.

Five. Make use of the Hawthorne effect. In the 1920s, some of the most famous industrial history experiments took place at Western Electric's factory in the Hawthorne suburb of Chicago. Lighting in the plant was manipulated to see if it would have any effect on worker productivity. The findings showed that each time the level of light was changed, productivity went up. Over the following decades, other variables were tested, including changes in the length of lunch breaks and workdays, which all resulted in the same positive impacts. These series of experiments led to what's now known as the Hawthorne effect, which is behavioral change in individuals in response to being observed or singled out for special treatment.

The ramifications of these experiments are especially relevant to effective business management today. As soon as you let employees know that you're going to be measuring their productivity, they become more efficient. They'll anticipate being tracked by straightening up immediately.

Some of the greatest names in process improvement have given their stamp of approval on this one, so you can rest assured it's a time-proven strategy that works. However, it does come with a distinct limitation. If you don't follow through with an effective monitoring system to measure what you intend to, you can make tremendous improvements in the short term that won't last. Your employees will eventually catch on and revert to their previous baseline. When that happens, you must address the slip up quickly, remind them that they're being watched and then implement a fully-automated, electronic system of measurement that works. Like magic they'll tighten up again. This time, it'll be for the long term.

I learned about the Hawthorne effect many years ago from people who were smarter than me. As one of the pioneers in healthcare data analysis, I personally use it to psychologically buy our leadership team time to fix inefficiencies in our medical practice. I periodically reveal to our employees that upper management is going to start digging deeper into their acute roles to better measure each individual's performance. Operations improve almost instantaneously. Everyone self corrects at an astounding rate. Then, as our people fall back into their old ways, we remind them of what we've implemented and show them their performance in terms of clearly-defined metrics. Once they realize we aren't bluffing, that we have a systematic process in place to keep watch, they usually maintain their improved performance.

Peter Drucker, world-renowned management consultant and educator, once said, "If you measure processes, they do get better." Simply communicating your intentions to do so will translate into substantial positive results, but they won't be long lasting unless you supplement your words with action. In short, if you want to help someone lose weight, start by buying them a scale.

"WHAT DO YOU HATE MOST ABOUT RUNNING A COMPANY?"

F iring someone is the worst situation. In my case, that means terminating a physician. It's a decision that I know will send ripples through all aspects of their life. Most times, if someone is underperforming at a specific task but has shown great passion and a willingness to work hard, you can move them around to more optimal positions that better suit their personality or skillset. If they're not willing to put in the effort or are incapable of learning from their mistakes, do what you must. It's never fun.

I don't keep people that have proven they can't do the job. Every member of our star-studded team at the lab have bought into this philosophy. We have developed a culture where everyone is willing to work hard because they know each individual is accountable for carrying their own weight. We respect each other's responsibility. If there's dead weight, we'll cut it, but it always elicits an unsettling feeling inside. I've never had a smile on my face while making that call.

"WHAT DO YOU LOVE MOST ABOUT RUNNING A COMPANY?"

My favorite part about running my own business is having the control to spend my time doing what I'm passionate about while surrounding myself with good people who are enjoyable to work alongside and that bring new ideas to the table. Between the meaningful work I get to pursue and the high-quality individuals I get to interact with, my mind continues to grow daily. That's a game changer that can be seen on the bottom line.

FIVE
LEAD FROM THE FRONT

"Our chief want is someone who will inspire us to be what we know we could be."
– Ralph Waldo Emerson

"A good plan violently executed now is better than a perfect plan executed next week" – George Patton

"Opportunity is missed by most people because it is dressed in overalls and looks like work."
– Thomas Edison

LEADERSHIP & FAME

I believe the world would be run by Nazis today if Winston Churchill didn't lead in the way he did during World War II. In 1940, Hitler decided to attack Britain from the sky. The Germans never set foot on British soil, but they bombed the hell out of the country. Churchill, the prime minister at the time, was a steadfast leader who motivated the British people when the Germans intensified their offensive. Each smoky night, he'd post up on the roof of his London bunker to witness the horrific destruction from the bombs that rained down from the sky, turning once cultural landmarks into concrete rubble. Fortunately, he was never struck by one. His fellow countrymen weren't so lucky. Following these spirit-crushing blood-baths, he'd reveal the damage inflicted by the Nazi aerial attacks and rally the resistance over the radio, urging the British to maintain their valiant efforts.

By June 1941, England was pretty much beaten into submission, but Churchill was determined to resist the Third Reich's conquest of his homeland. At that time, because they were already on the brink of defeat, and based on the size of Germany's army and comparative power, England could've been easily subdued by a swift land invasion. Hitler instead made a fateful decision that changed the course of history.

Churchill was relentless in reviving the hope of the British people following every destructive air raid. He had an iron will that I believe intimidated Hitler to his core. As history goes, Germany instead chose to invade Russia, which turned out to be a brick wall. Hitler bit off more than he could chew, spreading his army too thin, and everything fell apart for him shortly thereafter. John F. Kennedy made Churchill an honorary citizen of the United States for his heroics.

Not too long ago, I took a trip to Churchill's historic bunker and then visited his gravesite, which lays in a quaint English countryside. It was an awe-inspiring experience. Churchill was a phenomenal leader but elected to be buried unpretentiously in his rural family plot. There wasn't much more than the name on the headstone. Huge wreaths and flowers are still piled around him by reverent visitors, but it's nothing in comparison to U.S. presidents who are surrounded by ornate buildings and lavish spectacles. This was just a little old country church in a little old country cemetery. That's how he wanted to be remembered, or perhaps how he wanted to be forgotten.

I'm no history buff. Although I recognize there were admirable leaders before Winston Churchill, out of sight out of mind is how that works. The point is, Churchill wasn't fearlessly battling evil and suffering alongside his fellow countrymen for the sake of some post-mortem fame or an unknown stranger laying plastic flowers at his gravesite decades after his passing. Changing his country's then present circumstances by standing up for what he believed to be morally and justifiably right while saving the lives of the people he loved gave him deep-rooted feelings of self-worth and purpose that he could cherish for the rest of his days on Earth.

Fame is fleeting; it only lasts as long as people remember you. They tend to forget pretty quick. Once you and your immediate family pass on, your life becomes minor in the eyes of history. You're not going to be in the front of people's minds forever, so doing right by those around you and making a positive mark on the world while you're alive to see it will give you similar feelings of internal satisfaction that will last for at least the rest of your own lifetime. This is as close to eternal as we humans can get. When leaders recognize a problem, they aren't motivated by notoriety or accolades. Their goal is to impact, not impress. Leaders do things because they're necessary, not so they'll be remembered.

THE ANATOMY OF A LEADER

A nother impressive leader during the same period was General George Patton of the U.S. military. Patton was a workhorse who ferociously pursued the Nazis like a hunter. He couldn't be controlled by anyone, was unpredictable and often impulsive, which greatly intimidated the Germans. Patton's behavior also caused internal conflict among the U.S. command. In early 1943, during the Sicily Campaign, as Lieutenant General Patton was making rounds past the beds of his maimed and bleeding soldiers, he came across one man sprawled out on a cot. He stopped at the foot of the bed. This soldier had been diagnosed with psychoneurosis or "combat stress reaction". Without any visible injuries Patton didn't believe the man had any right to be treated at an evacuation hospital away from the front lines. He labeled the soldier a coward, verbally berated him and, in a fit of rage, struck the man's face. A week later he unleashed his fury on another unsuspecting soldier. Leaders are human; they make mistakes.

The media got word of the assaults, and they were widely publicized. Upon discovery of the incidents, Patton's superiors, General Dwight D. Eisenhower and Army Chief of Staff George Marshall, decided not to discharge him. Instead, they implemented a strategic suspension to the country's advantage. Shortly thereafter, false intelligence was sent to the Nazis that General Patton would be spearheading the invasion of Europe. Upper command then used him as a pawn by moving him around various countries to give a false indication of where the U.S. would likely attack from. The Germans meticulously tracked Patton's every move. They figured that if there was going to be any general leading the invasion, it was going to be him. As a result, the Nazi forces were scrambling leading up to D-Day. A leader is flexible and realizes an asset can be used in multiple ways.

My uncle was a distinctly older fellow when he enlisted in the U.S. military during World War II. Most of the soldiers were in their late teens or early twenties when they were drafted. My uncle was already twenty-nine, so he was immediately placed in Officer's Candidate School. Upon his graduation, he began training younger men moving up the ranks of the Tank Corp.

In 1944, the notorious Normandy Invasion, also known as D-Day, took place. Approximately 156,000 American, British, and Canadian soldiers landed on five beaches along the heavily fortified coast of France's Normandy region. Once the land was under Allied control, the tanks were let loose. My uncle rolled onto that beach, which looked like the dark entrance to the gates of hell, as a captain in the U.S. Tank Corp., shortly after the first wave of troops deployed. All the soldiers went in knowing the odds of them walking out of there alive were low, but they had a job to do.

After the Allied forces made initial headway into Europe, with the onset of winter in December of 1944, the German army launched a surprise blitzkrieg counteroffensive in the Ardennes region of Belgium, known as the Battle of the Bulge. This was one of Hitler's last great attempts to turn the tide of the war. The U.S. Army responded to the deadly threat by unleashing General Patton back into the battle as head of the U.S. Tank Corp. Once that reintroduction happened, my uncle was directly under Patton's command. He told me that the fearless general led the charge with his subordinates on the front lines. He led from the front. Patton cut through enemy territory like a hot knife through butter, making the Germans quiver in their boots every step of the way. Winston Churchill later coined the crucial victory as "the greatest American battle of the war."

My uncle fought all across Europe. Miraculously he survived, but he came back with invisible scars to show for it. He witnessed the most disgusting human atrocities during his time there, including being one of the first liberators on the scene of the horrific Nazi prison camps. Most soldiers kept the gruesome details of what they experienced to themselves. My uncle was no exception. However, he did mention one especially haunting memory. While the Allied forces were liberating various European cities, General Patton expressed to his tankers that if they received one stray bullet of enemy fire, they had an immediate green light to flatten the city. My uncle prayed that no sorry soul would be foolish enough to provoke his platoon. He understood full well what the deadly ramifications would be for doing so. In the cobblestone streets of a picturesque French village, his platoon of tankers was shot at. The reaction was instantaneous. His tankers decimated the once bustling town square to shrapnel and black soot. It was a decision that bothered my uncle for the rest of his life. Still, he and Patton knew why they had joined the fight for freedom and what they were willing to sacrifice to win the Second World War. If you ever saw the movie, *Band of Brothers*, that's the most realistic presentation I've seen. It's a tough decision to give the order to destroy an entire village, or to be the individual to pull the trigger, but as a leader you have to understand your why, to assess the best route to the desired goal, and to be decisive when everything is up in the air. Once you establish yourself as a leader, you must have the resilience to remain in the fight, the discipline to stay true to your principles, and the courage to act when the battle breaks out. Leaders persevere.

We've had plenty of low moments in our pathology group, but we never flatlined. Our leadership team constantly reassessed the direction in which we were moving, and at times, we were faced with picking the best of all rotten options to keep our momentum. We chose decisively, coordinated our efforts, and persevered until we achieved our strategic goals. I've come to find that nothing in life ever goes exactly to plan. Your ability to lead will ultimately depend on how successful you are at maneuvering yourself and your team through challenging situations. Anyone can lead when life is easy. It's how you act while dragging your boots through the muck of tough times that splits the men and women from the boys and girls. When I look back at each down moment, it was clear our leadership team had worked tirelessly to get back to a positive baseline. Simple as that. Nothing held us down for long, and the employees following our lead never forgot it.

Leadership often requires taking a position that isn't fully supported by those around you at times when you aren't even completely sure of the outcome. It's about acknowledging uncertainty yet taking a firm stance based on previous experience or advice from those you trust, rather than a sheer guess. As a leader, if you feel strongly about something, you have to do your research, take calculated risks, and persevere until you reach your goal.

The anatomy of a leader includes a flexible core able to withstand the unpredictable blows that life constantly wields. It includes powerful arms and legs to regain stability and move forward decisively when everything seems to be going wrong. Finally, the anatomy of a leader includes a cool head and an open mind that is humble enough to deal with whatever the consequences may be.

LEADERSHIP & ACHIEVEMENT

The most successful leaders understand who they are and what they're about. They stand for something. They have high standards. They aren't going to cut corners to make a quick buck. They're always going to consider how their actions will affect those around them and the success of the overarching mission. In other words, the journey they take to the end destination matters just as much as actually reaching it. Through the process, these leaders cement unbreakable relationships with crucial allies, and allies drive achievement. The highest achievers are also able to retain the talent they attract by staying true to their principles while preserving the interests of those following their lead.

If you put our employees' careers under a microscope, one thing you'll notice is that once they join, they rarely ever leave. I can't tell you how many that've retired within the last ten years — I've been here over forty, so there's been a few — who started their careers with us. We've developed deep relationships that've even extended to some of their children. Now all grown up, several have joined, making us a multi-generational organization.

This dynamic is highly unusual nowadays. As I previously mentioned, individuals often have an underwhelming loyalty toward their employer because companies let their people go when times get tough. I hire employees knowing full well they'll have their ups and downs. When they do experience the adverse cycles of life, I'm prepared to help them emerge to a more prosperous state. Even your top performers will experience their own unique struggles that come with human life, be it personal insecurities, death, divorce, serious illness, and God knows what else. As a leader, you need to have foresight and help your team through these dark times when the easy solution is to sever ties and move on. It's how I look at the world. Recruiting top quality pros is a daunting task. Once you finally align a few with your mission, it's worthwhile to keep them. In turbulent times give them the encouragement to get back on their feet. That may be the lift they need to stand tall. My people helped lift me to where I am today.

You need to look at all the people around you, especially during the adverse times, and analyze the impact you're making on them. That's the true measure of how well you've done as a leader and an indication of your future achievement. At the medical lab Dr. Minielly and I established, we've had some employees working with us for almost five decades. During our last annual celebration to honor them, we asked these individuals what kept them around for so long. What may come as a surprise to you is that an overwhelming majority answered by recounting an onerous situation that occurred over the prior twelve months as opposed to a surface-level positive formality. Our response in the wake of their toughest life challenges remained clearest in their minds. Some appreciated our leadership team for meeting their needs during a specific down moment. Others expressed gratefulness for the overall job security they experienced throughout their employment, especially during the turbulent periods in their personal lives. This allowed them to properly educate their kids, successfully raise a family, and take some exciting vacations along the way.

Your greatest value as a leader is being able to deal with challenges and solve problems that others on your team are either unwilling or incapable of overcoming. Refrain from doing what's expedient during trying times when it relates to the important people in your organization. Instead, try to find solutions for them.

One of the things Dr. Minielly and I noticed when we first started at St. John Health System was that there were a lot of individuals at the company working as janitors, custodians, cleaning crew, and others, whose families would be disproportionately affected by a lost job or pay cut. These individuals performed the less glamourous, yet vital, behind-the-scenes work that kept our organization operating smoothly. It dawned on us that many of these people were living on the edge, holding on by a mere thread. We witnessed a heartbreaking situation where an employee's child got injured, tragically passed away, and their family lacked the financial means of burying them. As a leader, once you become aware of a glaring problem affecting the important people you care about, address the issue with flexibility. Give a hand to those who need it rather than turning a blind eye.

The hand Dr. Minielly and I extended came in the form of a fund we set up at the St. John Foundation, called the Employee Disaster Fund. We made sure it was an easily accessible resource for the HR team to distribute. It's been left completely up to their discretion to determine the response to each situation they face. From the beginning, we've made it a point to donate anonymously. The partners in our group have contributed about $80,000 a year since 1980. Because of the positive impact it's had on our employees, whenever the account is used up, I'll make some calls to have it topped off. This helping hand has incidentally been returned in organizational cooperation, employee loyalty, and the achievement of our strategic goals, but we never aimed to get a benefit out of it. There was a detrimental problem affecting the wellbeing of those we cared about. Whether or not we were recognized as the ones who brought a solution to the table, and regardless of any reward we might've received, it was the right thing to do.

The highest achievers live by one of the most powerful principles: help yourself by helping others. What you give always comes back in one form or another. It's not always in a monetary equivalent, but often in loyal allies, immense respect, and new opportunities. This is how to lead a winning team for five decades.

"WHO IS THE MOST IMPRESSIVE LEADER YOU'VE MET OUTSIDE OF YOUR FAMILY, AND WHAT DID YOU LEARN FROM THEM?"

Most of them are dead now because I've been at this for so long. There was one individual I got to know during the 1990s who comes to mind. His name isn't important, what matters is his background. He was an investor that established small banks, merged them with others, and then, over a period of time, he'd sell the chain to a larger banking institution. This man took on tremendous risk but was able to guide his investments and various companies through murky waters. He was an immensely experienced leader who overcame plenty of challenges during his lifetime. He made some brilliant decisions, and some dumb ones, which he would never shy away from sharing with me. My investor friend was on the board of the same hospital system as me, so we'd grab lunch every other month. We started building rapport while he considered different tactics relating to his parenting strategy. I had three children of my own, so whenever he would ask for my thoughts, I'd share my personal experience. In return, I'd ask him for financial advice.

By the end of his life, my friend had amassed quite a bit of wealth. With a brewing passion for helping the less fortunate members of our community, he started moving his assets around. He only revealed bits and pieces of his plans, but it was enough to get my wheels turning. Over a corned beef sandwich one day, I proposed a solution that would bridge his philanthropic interests with a real community need. I explained, "We should form an organization that helps our at-risk schools in poor areas. They're not going to survive unless someone steps in." I captivated his interest. Following our conversation, I came across an article in a business magazine that highlighted what a Baltimore organization had done for the Catholic schools in its local parishes. I tore out the article and slapped it on the table next time we spoke. That's how we came up with the name Friends of the Catholic Education.

From a business standpoint, the entire Catholic school system in our city was structured inefficiently. We came up with the idea to completely re-organize it. The system needed to have fewer schools, to put more money into the ones that were retained, and to develop higher quality staff. Many of the schools still had nuns teaching. The organizational issue of the Catholic school system was a philosophical one. At the time, Tulsa had two centralized Catholic high schools and numerous decentralized grade schools associated with the various parishes. Our idea was to consolidate all the grade schools into a few larger institutions that could run more efficiently. To our dismay, that plan didn't fly well with the bishop, nor with the members of the various parishes. Re-structuring it that way was quickly off the table. We had to attack the problem from a different angle.

While my friend and I continued to mull over our options, he and his daughter went to survey St. Catherine grade school. This school was part of a poor parish to the north of us, in the lower echelon of Tulsa, a place that wasn't looked on approvingly by the public. My investor friend walked away from his visit and confirmed, "This school has potential, but it isn't going to survive unless we give them financial support. Let's set up a foundation. I'll help fund it, and we'll also have campaigns every year to maximize the dollars coming in." I agreed to invest in the cause, and we rounded up a few other leaders with deep pockets to join us as well. Two of them even decided to match all donations received.

One of the problems with a Catholic education is that it must be privately funded. In wealthy neighborhoods that wasn't a problem because the parents were able to cover the cost of a premium education. In poorer neighborhoods like the one where St. Catherine was located, although many parents might've wanted to send their kids to a Catholic school, they simply couldn't afford it. They were essentially barred from the private option entirely. As a result, St. Catherine had low admissions and inadequate revenue to cover its overhead expenses. Our solution was to provide scholarship money to hardworking families so they could cover the pricey tuition. This would also help the school improve their teaching staff. We intended to level the playing field.

This co-founding partner of mine has since passed away, but his daughter continues to hold a leadership role in the foundation. To be clear, we aren't interested in bailing out schools with a lump sum payment. That's a one-time deal. Instead, our goal is to create a steady source of reliable income that these institutions can depend on for the long term. The families pay whatever they can manage, and we make up the difference, or they don't pay anything, and we cover it all. We want the children to receive a quality education so they can live an independent life and become contributing members of the community. Our hope is that once they are all grown up, out making a living, they'll pass on the help they received to someone else who needs it.

Today, we support four schools through Friends of the Catholic Education. Their admissions have steadily increased. St. Catherine had fifty students when we started. Now that number hovers around 160. It's a nicely fenced, secure little school in the heart of an insecure neighborhood. The teachers who keep the whole operation running could certainly use their talent to do financially better elsewhere, but they're determined to make a difference close to home. I recently attended a homeroom class and was blown away by how the teacher was able to captivate her students' attention. She called each child by name and skillfully guided them through their lessons with a vibrant energy that kept the whole class engaged until the recess bell rang. That was a miracle in itself. My grandchildren ended up attending St. Catherine. It was good for them to realize how unstable many other children's lives were. They didn't have it too bad after all.

As you achieve success, you'll begin to realize that there were always people supporting you along the way. I've worked hard and taken the necessary risks to become successful, but I was never an island. Once you find yourself in a position to pass on the blessings you received, it's important to reach down into the trench and help pull someone out. Some will grip on to the lifeline. Some will leave you hanging. Offer the hand anyway. Developing a personal interest in helping others has added new meaning to my life. The charity I offer is somewhat based on my innate selfishness. Making the world a better place for others makes it better for me. In other words, I largely help people because it makes me feel good. After you gift someone a hand through tough times, stop and see how *you* feel.

A liberating personal goal is to live well every day. I've found that this boils down to a feeling that comes from helping others live well. Money is an impactful tool of choice. I learned a lot from this impressive individual who was instrumental in founding Friends of the Catholic Education. He helped me realize a higher purpose to acquiring wealth.

THE GREAT EQUALIZER

My parents taught me that a strong work ethic is the surest way to career and life success. I may have lacked self confidence in my youth, but I was motivated and held down a job starting from sixteen years old. I continued to work through high school, college, and even during medical school. Although my father earned an average income, we didn't have an excessive amount of money. I needed to make something on the side to fulfill my dreams. I've worked a long time to build my success. Believe it or not, I still enjoy what I do. A tenacious work ethic was embedded in me by my parents and various jobs. Now it's inseparable from my nature.

At eighty-five years of age, I still spend an ungodly amount of time working, for the most part in my pathology practice. This challenging work drives me to get up in the morning and fills me with a youthful energy that has delayed the deterioration of my mind and body. I derive meaning from what I do. I also understand, now more than ever, the importance of slowing down to watch a movie with my wife, visiting a friend, or enjoying a weekend getaway with my family. You have to find a balance between working like hell and enjoying the countryside at times, but always stay engaged. That's how to keep life pumping through your veins.

Most people think of work as an emotional and physical energy suck, but real enjoyment can come from doing *purposeful* work. This is simply a matter of discovering the right kind of challenge that turns the pursuit of victory into a full-fledged obsession. That's my definition of passion. Mix in a bit of that with an indomitable work ethic and you'll be able to achieve even your highest goals.

The mindset that led me to great achievement is centered on the following belief. You may be smarter than me, but you cannot and will not outwork me. Work rate has always been my edge. Success isn't just about brains, intelligence, education, or being the most talented. Although they can certainly help, they aren't prerequisites, and none of them can replace the impact of hard work. Anyone can work hard; only a few do. Will you?

LEAD A TEAM OF WORKHORSES

Assembling a team of hard workers will facilitate effective leadership. Surrounding yourself with a team that lacks this crucial attribute will leave you dead in your tracks. If your team is failing to achieve results, evaluate your personnel. You may find a gap in the roster that needs to be filled or a poor performer that needs to be replaced.

Some people lack the self-discipline to work hard. They won't commit to a project or burn the midnight oil to see it through. They may seem to be competent and adequately skilled yet consistently fail to complete their tasks on time. Some people aren't willing to sacrifice the lesser pleasures to reach the greater end. On the other hand, there are those who always complete the tedious yet important tasks without complaint. The individuals that keep their head down and diligently work hard toward a group's collective goals. Judging an individual's work ethic is crucial to assembling and leading a winning team to lasting success and future achievement.

This year our pathology group assimilated several veteran workhorses that were on the brink of being let go from our health system during a corporate downsize. Although it caused some internal conflict initially, this has since become one of the best decisions our group has ever made. Ascension is the parent company that oversees St. John Health System. A few years ago, Ascension created the vision that St. John was going to house some of their primary laboratory assets nationwide. To make that a reality, the health system had to hire additional management personnel. A few years later, Ascension curbed their plans and decided their Tulsa laboratory was too top heavy. To trim the ranks, they implemented various staffing formulas that dictated how many people could be under one manager and then reduced the total number of positions. As a result, some of the health system's most experienced players, who had worked there between ten and twenty years, were set to have their roles terminated. It was up to each of those individuals to reapply for the remaining roles. The problem was these weren't starry-eyed rookies. They didn't have to stay. They could've just as easily worked elsewhere or retired altogether.

The system was going to lose five experienced professionals. It was to our pathology group's advantage to bring them into our elite team, regardless of the political consequences for doing so. At first, the existing partners in the group weren't convinced it was the right move. Everyone was wondering what the hell I was doing, questioning whether I had completely lost my marbles. Sometimes you have to take calculated risks. Not everyone will agree with you, but if you develop confidence and trust ahead of time, your team will give you the benefit of the doubt more often than not. I just couldn't fathom letting such experienced hard workers clear out their desks.

In our group, we've always had non-medical management professionals to help the organization run smoothly on the back end. Our CFO has a strictly financial role, and our COO's background is in technology. Under these executives, we have several directors responsible for various business and administrative activities. These were the roles we filled. It was a big payroll to take on, but we did have three pathologists retiring at that time. The ironic thing is that we didn't even end up needing to refill those specialized positions. With the new management personnel, we had the ability to change how we operated. Our directors oversee complex aspects of the organization, including fine-tuning the revenue cycle and billing system, which continues to make our pathologists' workday more efficient. As a result, our collection rate increased by 10 percent that year. We were able to handle the higher volume with fewer people. These managers paid back a return and then some of the cost that it took to assimilate them into the group. I went out on a limb, but it made sense because I knew they were capable workhorses.

One of the most alarming problems I was battling with, prior to the addition of these directors, was that none of the current pathologists in the group wanted to take my place upon my retirement. I understood the hesitancy. In a position like mine, you get so involved in the business side of things that you lose some of your pathology skills. No one was willing to sacrifice that. Now with our new additions, the team is well equipped to charge on without me. If you have hard-working and experienced people following your lead, get out of their way so they can do their job. You'll be surprised by what they can accomplish. The king is dead. Long live the corporation.

PART THREE

A COMPREHENSIVE APPROACH TO INVESTMENT

Side note from Terry:

T he goal of Part Three is to arm you with the investment principles that have created financial abundance in my life. What I've personally accomplished isn't important. I only mention snapshots of my experience to teach lessons and illustrate the results of my greater philosophy. Consult with your own experts before making any financial decisions.

SIX
GUIDING INVESTMENT PRINCIPLES

Bezos: "Your investment thesis is so simple. You're the second richest guy in the world, and it's so simple. Why doesn't everyone just copy you?"

Buffett: "Because nobody wants to get rich slow."

FULL POCKETS, STORMY MARKETS

My investment journey began when I left the Mayo Clinic for private practice in Kansas City in the early 1970s. The market was stormy. Until 1980, it was tough to make any money in the stock market. Brokers were losing their jobs, Wall Street was on its back, and public sentiment was pessimistic. This was a time characterized by stagflation in the country, meaning prices were inflating while the economy continued to depress further, the worst of all economic scenarios. The oil embargo was also at play, which led to massive lines of people frantically waiting to refill their gas tanks. The aftermath of the COVID-19 pandemic and the Russian War in Ukraine that we are currently traversing is difficult; however, history has seen down cycles in the past that were similarly disquieting.

Since it was a bear stock market, and I was working in a private medical practice, just beginning to bring home some heavy paychecks, I turned to alternative investments that proved more resilient to the economic climate. One asset, abundant in Kansas City, captivated my interest. Farmland wasn't priced too expensively, and crops were profitable. I felt it had a safe future, so I decided to take a chance on real estate.

At the time, I was a young physician working near Smithville, Missouri. This was an intimate town to the north of Kansas City, where everyone was on a first-name basis. As an outsider, I didn't know everyone personally, but my name was familiar in the community due to my reputation as an established member of a prominent pathology group. Eventually, I got to know a senior farmer who was ready to retire. This man was looking to fund the remaining years of his life by selling his fully paid off farm property. I struck a deal to take it off his hands. Because he considered me a safe debt risk, he agreed to personally carry the note that I could pay off at any time in an installment sale, also known as seller financing. In other words, I gave the farmer a modest cash down payment initially and then he loaned me the remaining amount of the purchase price, which I agreed to pay back to him over time. This meant that I didn't have to obtain a conventional mortgage from a bank. More importantly, it freed me from having to tie up a bunch of money up front. This kept me liquid when most of the nation was strapped for cash. As a side note, many owners in or nearing retirement prefer to receive a steady cash stream in smaller monthly installments, as opposed to a single lump sum payment. It allows them to spread out their tax hit on the gains.

This turned out to be a great deal for the both of us, and my growing family later built a home on the land we had purchased. What evolved over time, at this stage of my investment career, was a strong interest in real estate. This was the first domino to fall.

PROCEEDS

As you may recall, around this time Dr. Minielly and I wrote Neal Patterson a check to keep his consultancy from becoming insolvent before our proprietary laboratory software was released. In return for our risky investment, we received a portion of company stock when it later went public under the Cerner brand. Investing directly in the technology giant was never part of my plan. My primary motivation was designing a robust medical program that would bolster my lab strategy. For ethical reasons, I decided to pay the long-term capital gains tax and cash out my shares just a few years later.

My pockets were full heading into the late 1980s, early 1990s, in an economy that was just beginning to recover from the bloodbath of the prior decade. I had already moved to Tulsa to establish an outreach laboratory testing business on behalf of St. John Health System, and I took out a loan to build my family a permanent home on a new spacious plot of land. The market was heating up. Everyone was trying to hit a quick home run.

People tend to make bad decisions when they lack experience and perspective. I was young, but I knew the decision of how to spend my waterfall would dictate the trajectory of my investment career. Did I have the option to take out more debt to purchase new toys and investments all at once? Absolutely. Did I do that? No. I personally walked away with about $2 million after cashing out my Cerner stock and used the proceeds to pay down every penny of debt under my name. I managed my pot of gold effectively, which sent the rest of my investment career into overdrive.

THE HEART

My general investment philosophy is to borrow conservatively and invest carefully. As soon as the right time comes to capitalize on the gains, I secure the profit. Then I take the proceeds and clear my debt immediately before reinvesting in any other assets. Looking back over my history, I've repeated this pattern numerous times. I held some investments long term where it made sense, but I was also never concerned about paying the capital gains taxes from cashing out in the short term during a hot market in order to lower my debt load. This strategy allowed me to steadily increase my net worth while minimizing my leverage risk. I never add debt to debt like the majority do, particularly in real estate. This is the heart of my overarching investment philosophy.

Take my prior investment in Missouri farmland, for example. I borrowed, in the form of seller financing, to purchase a property for a good deal in a down market. Then I improved the plot of land with a newly built house and held the asset for a few years. Once the market turned around, I opted to pay the capital gains tax, realize my profits, and eliminate my other debts immediately. Finally, I waited until pricing was more affordable before reinvesting what was left over into more land as well as other high-performing assets at the time. I was disciplined and methodical as I scaled up, always devising a plan for the proceeds before moving any money around.

Become a principled investor and your wealth will compound swiftly and effortlessly. Lose focus, divert from the fundamentals, or practice whimsical gut-feeling betting, and accumulating wealth will be a long and strenuous endeavor. Warren Buffett explains just how this dynamic works in life and investment in his biography, *The Snowball: Warren Buffett and the Business of Life*, by Alice Schroeder, when he says,

Life is like a snowball. The important thing is to find wet snow and a really long hill . . . The snowball just happens if you're in the right kind of snow, and that's what happened with me. I don't just mean compounding money either. It's in terms of understanding the world and what kind of friends you accumulate. You get to select over time, and you've got to be the kind of person that the snow wants to attach itself to. You've got to be your own wet snow, in effect. You'd better be picking up snow as you go along, because you're not going to be getting back up to the top of the hill again. That's the way life works.

CASE 1.0 – THE DOC STRUCK A VEIN, OF OIL

O il was undoubtedly my toughest investment, but I enjoyed the thrill of the ride. Through the late 1900s, the price of oil was almost exclusively determined by external forces, constantly manipulated by individuals with immense political power. In other words, prices were set by the Middle East. An oil company was, therefore, subject to the international oil whims, which could drop the price per barrel at any moment. Less control for an owner is risky business. It's also much harder to add value to a commodity investment like oil. This asset has its drawbacks; however, I'm always open to a favorable deal.

The two other physician partners that I originally got involved in the oil and gas business with, during the late 1970s, were my good friends Dr. John Minielly and Dr. Bill Sheehan. We stuck the first initial of each of our last names together to create the moniker DMS Investments. In 1980, the notorious oil embargo slashed the price of U.S. oil. In just two years, around the beginning of 1982, oil had dropped to a mere nine dollars a barrel, significantly lower than the recent historical average. My partners had seen enough damage and opted for an exit. I, on the other hand, have always been interested in acquiring assets at a discount during temporary downturns with a belief that the investment will become much more valuable upon its stabilization in a positive market upswing. I decided to stay with it and increase my stake.

In my experience, the most valuable investments arise in the dreariest of times. The investors who save money while the sun is shining can capitalize on the opportunities that manifest out of storms that roar through the market. The recessionary storm of the 1980s is a perfect example. Oil prices plummeted from sky high to rock bottom incredibly fast. Once prices dwindled below the cost of production, it didn't take a rocket scientist to piece together the outcome. After my partners pulled their capital out of the market, I came across some promising oil wells formerly owned by a company that had since gone bankrupt. I understood oil to be a cyclical business by nature, with years of ups and downs, and that buying low was the golden opportunity to make money when it inevitably turned. I was confident that eventually it would. I bailed out the company, acquired a few additional oil leases and started improving its operations in the early 1980s. Although the deal looked good on paper, actually managing a company during that period was extremely difficult. It was impossible to do alone. Luckily, I was able to hire a talented geologist who was out of work, an operator with thirty years of industry experience who had been laid off, and I even recruited my son to help facilitate the turnaround. We then subcontracted out the drilling and workover rigs as needed.

In the oil and gas industry, after a company identifies a promising well to drill on, it will usually turn to outside investors for support in funding it. Often, unintentionally, the investors get somewhat screwed over with excessive fees and risk. The capital partners I would have turned to were primarily medical professionals. I didn't feel comfortable including them in such risky investments, especially ones they weren't fully educated on, regardless of how high the upside could be. If I drilled on what turned out to be a dry hole, I would've felt directly responsible for their sunk cost.

At the same time, our team wasn't wild catting, meaning drilling where there weren't any previously identified wells. An oil lease is a legal contract between a landowner and an oil company that gives the company the right to explore for oil on a specified plot of land. For each of the leases we took over, we targeted specific wells that had already been partially drilled, focusing the bulk of our efforts on specific sites that we believed still had untapped oil reserves. All the historical information was recorded in the state's oil and gas records, which allowed our team to make educated guesses on where the hidden profits were. Before ever breaking ground, we knew how deep the previous operator had drilled and what zones they hit at those depths. Our geologist had the fun challenge of comparing all the known wells on our lease with the information recorded by the state to identify which were full of promise and which were busts. Sometimes we struck gold, other times barely broke even, but the tax write-offs ultimately incentivized us to keep drilling.

The oil and gas industry had special privileges relating to the tax code to entice people to take on the excessive risk of drilling. It was geared to benefit the investor, but the downside risk was still significant. In those days, we didn't have limited liability companies, so I structured the business as a c-corporation. I was legally considered the "sole investor" because I personally funded all the operations, even though I also retained complete ownership of the company that was using the money. This allowed me to maximize the depreciation benefits.

Depreciation write-offs in the oil business were short, three to five years back then. The way it worked was I'd personally fund the operations and then my company would carry out the drilling work. We would service a well together for a max of five years, or until it was fully depreciated, at which point I'd capitalize ownership from myself, as the sole investor, back to the c-corporation. This would reset the depreciation cycle once again for the corporate entity. Along with the double depreciation write-offs, I also received additional tax credits and deductions I was able to use against my taxable income for a long time, which came as a pleasant surprise.

Each lease we owned gave us the right to explore approximately twenty wells. As long as we actively serviced one of them, we could maintain the entire lease. However, every well didn't produce the same amount of oil. As we started running into deficiencies with the parts on our machines, we began swapping them out of the wells that produced the smallest amount of oil and putting them to work on our few cash cows, the ones with the greatest upside potential. At one point, because of how many parts we were shifting around, we only had five wells actively producing oil, with the rest left idle. We had to be selective over the years, but it allowed us to avoid mounting debt obligations. For over twenty years, our team serviced a total of 160 to 170 wells. We never borrowed outside of my own bank account to do it. Admittedly, even if I wanted to take out a loan against the oil company, I couldn't. No lender would've granted one while the industry was down on its back. That turned out to be a good thing. Debt was a complexity we didn't need. Avoiding it decreased our risk.

Despite money and parts being tight, we were always able to pay the salaries of our employees. The individuals that operated our drilling rigs loved to do business with us because they knew we would pay them, something that only a few other owners could say at the time. As a result, we had excellent cooperation out in the field. With the strong reputation we built, the players of our industry respected us. That allowed us to function very efficiently.

Actively working a well was exhilarating. The steel drills would grind down through hard rock for twenty-four hours straight while the geologists collected ground material samples to evaluate the zones we were in. We tracked their progress with intense anticipation down to a max depth of 4,000 feet. I never followed the lead of other large operators who drilled down 18,000 feet in some of the mammoth wells. If something were to break down, we would've had the fun task of ripping the pump and tube, 40 feet at a time, out of the well to fix it. After the repair, we would've then had to drop it right back down again one piece at a time. We stayed within our means, so the business was manageable.

Eventually it became too costly to produce the oil. With my son's enjoyment withering from all the financial ups and downs, we planned an exit. In a way, your investment has to match your personality. The volatility of oil was too risky for his blood. Our company scraped by in the 1980s and built momentum in the 1990s. Once the market came roaring back in the early 2000s, with the price of oil at forty dollars a barrel, we sold on the upswing to a private company. That's the nature of the oil business. It's feast or famine, but when it's feast, boy, it's big-time dollars. We held out for over twenty years until the right opportunity to sell arrived during a hot market. Although we didn't sell DMS Investments at the very top, we realized a significant profit that covered all our costs and then some. Be that as it may, I realized other businesses would allow us to run more efficiently. I had my sights set on real estate, which was far more predictable.

Rather than a standard cash out sale, in this situation we executed a 1031 exchange. This refers to the Internal Revenue Code's section 1031, which is a tax incentive that allows a real estate owner to defer paying capital gains taxes that would normally be charged at closing by immediately rolling all the proceeds from the sold property into the acquisition of new "like kind" property. Because an oil lease is considered a type of land lease, which is real estate in Oklahoma, I deposited the proceeds in a trust account monitored by a third-party intermediary and used the funds to purchase my first commercial real estate buildings. This minimized the capital gains taxes I had to pay on the profits. It generally makes sense to execute a 1031 exchange in a long-term real estate investment, but if for some reason I couldn't do a 1031 or didn't want to do one, I wouldn't hesitate to pay the price of safely cashing out and eliminating my debt. This is just one of many ways to get to the same end result.

CASE 2.0 – VACATION HOMES FOR INVESTMENT AND ENJOYMENT

Note from the author:

nvestment and enjoyment aren't diametrically opposed ideas. It's possible to enjoy relaxing days in a mountain cabin, lake house, or beach bungalow while simultaneously making a generous profit off the properties. Here's how Terry did it.

Dr. Terrence Dolan: In the early 2000s, after our kids graduated college, my wife and I had what seemed like ample free time. We reintroduced ourselves. Our desire to travel led us on a ten-day journey through the misty Blue Ridge Mountains of Tennessee. We enjoyed immersing ourselves in the breathtaking landscape so much that we returned several times over the following years. After a handful of visits, Mary Beth and I decided to switch it up. We zeroed in on a place that we'd briefly stopped through on the way to a few horse shows some years back. We packed up our motor home and headed west on Highway 50, a straight route to Gunnison, Colorado. Without concrete plans once we arrived at our final destination, we made a local mobile home park our main base, rented a Jeep, and took off to conquer the mountains. My wife and I couldn't get enough of the wilderness solitude and illuminating sunsets. For how often we visited, we started considering what it would cost to buy land.

When mountain property is up, it's worth a fortune. When it's down, the value plummets. It's a tricky market. I came across three developer brothers who owned 4,500 acres of land far up in the Colorado mountains. They had audacious plans to build and sell what was at that time very lucrative property. A turbulent market curbed their plans. After the brothers' development slowed with the local economy, they were motivated to liquidate some of their assets. I could smell opportunity, and fortunately, I reached out at the right time. I bought the first thirty-five-acre lot at the highest elevation along a winding creek, with scenic views of the mountain range. The property was worth what we paid at the time, but we had our work cut out for us to transform the blank dirt canvas into a fully inhabitable living arrangement. We wrote a few line items into the purchase contract to account for that. Everything is a negotiation.

Mountain living poses two primary risks. First is the flood potential. Following a fresh dump of powdery snowfall, if a heat wave passes through the mountain range too soon, it could melt the snowpack, causing the entire valley to flood. Although we saw the water level rise out of our creek bed, it never materially affected us because as part of the deal we had agreed that the developers would raise our lot five feet. We also built into the contract that the brothers would develop a drivable road into our property, bring power to the lot, and drill a well for us. This wasn't my first time living out in the country, so I was comfortable getting my water the old-fashioned way. The latter contingency turned out to be a great deal in and of itself. The well took three failed attempts to finally get right. I was only obligated to pay a quarter of the last effort. The rest of the cost was on the developers' dime.

If you decide to live in the mountains, the second risk to mitigate is the wildfire potential. I took it upon myself to tear out every pine tree within one hundred feet of where our motorhome was parked. We continued our project by installing a septic system for sewage. The final piece of the puzzle was a deal I struck with a local soft water company to rent a purification device. I considered this property an investment and an opportunity for leisure. I needed to have all the necessities at my fingertips. When my wife and I rolled into town, all we had to do was connect the sewage disposal and the power hookup to our motorhome, and it was vacation time. For the first couple years, Mary Beth and I simply parked the RV on the dirt lot and kicked back. That was enough.

I always kept my eye on the home values in the area. Because we were travelling there so often, it eventually made sense to sell the motorhome and upgrade to a permanent ATV riding, creek bed swimming, rolling hill cabin getaway. We built a 4,000-square-foot home that had a cozy crackling fireplace, a giant chandelier made of deer antlers over the dining room table, and a wood interior finished with a smooth gloss that gave the effect of a swanky lodge nestled into the mountainside.

Our family spent twenty thrilling years in Colorado, but it was an arduous trip to get there. With our young grandchildren in the back seat, we got tired of hearing "Are we there yet?" on repeat. Truthfully, it was a pain for all of us. During the ski season there were a few direct American Airlines flights to Gunnison, but there was only an indirect flight offered in summertime, which made flying just as much of a time suck as the thirteen-hour drive. Although we shared some unforgettable memories in Gunnison, our collective interest in the destination dwindled each time we had to make the burdensome journey out there. My other concern was that our house was sitting at an elevation of 8,100 feet, with our wilderness area extending up to 9,100 feet. At the time, my wife and I didn't have any problems handling that from a pulmonary heart standpoint, but I knew that, as we got older, some complications could potentially arise.

The good news was, by that point, the property had appreciated significantly from our continued improvements. The overall economy had also come full circle. Essentially, we were sitting on an extremely valuable asset that was hardly being used. That didn't make a whole lot of sense, so we decided it was the right time to put it on the market. This was one of the most enjoyable investments I have ever owned. It returned our family a hefty profit that we were ultimately able to roll into another deal that I will elaborate on in the next section.

The key to a successful vacation home investment is to get your timing right. Buy when the market is down and sell when it rebounds, flying high. To execute this strategy effectively, you must understand the supply and demand trends of the local market in which you're operating. You also have to diligently save capital in its most liquid form. Finally, it's imperative that you perform your due diligence on the acute risks of each specific property before making a final move. Eventually, profitable opportunities will reveal themselves, and you will be ready to take advantage.

CASE 2.1 – VACATION HOMES FOR INVESTMENT AND ENJOYMENT

A longtime friend of mine, who lived across the ridge in Gunnison, developed a life-threatening cancer before we sold our mountain home. He was initially seen by a urologist in a small Western Colorado community. After he broke the news to us, Mary Beth and I paid a trip to the hospital to see him. My friend couldn't give me a clear indication of what the issues were, so I requested his permission to analyze the tissue myself. I needed to know what we were dealing with. I huddled up with the pathologists working his case and examined the sample. Walking out of the lab, I understood that my friend was at the wrong hospital. He needed to receive treatment from a larger institution with greater capability. He didn't have the faintest idea of where to go. I had just the place in mind.

This man had done well for himself financially and owned a second home in Scottsdale, Arizona, conveniently located near a Mayo Clinic. Lightbulb. Whenever you run into a complex medical situation, you need to seek treatment from a place that's equipped for the battle. The Mayo Clinic was geared to handle his daunting case. The problem was my friend wasn't a member. I told him I'd handle it. Anyone can be referred through the Mayo Clinic's online process, so I made a few calls and emphasized the need for an urgent evaluation based on his malignant biopsy. He had an appointment within a week.

As it turned out, my friend required a serious surgical operation. Because he had a small family, we decided to go down and support him. I remained by his bedside throughout the postoperative care to translate the technical medical jargon in a way that would allow him to truly understand what the heck was going on in his body. My wife stopped by periodically in between shopping through the many for sale properties that had sprouted up in the aftermath of the 2008 housing crisis. When the economy went to pot in 2008, the city of Scottsdale was hemorrhaging, and my wife discovered an opportunity to buy a beautiful home nearby. I negotiated with the seller to knock the price down by 30 percent because the buyer had all the leverage at the time. The house came completely furnished, even the bedding was included. Additionally, due to the fact that so many people were out of work, we were able to hire extremely capable individuals to renovate the place. Slowly and steadily, we added value to our investment. For seven years we enjoyed relaxing desert trips with friends and family.

In highly desirable cities like Scottsdale, Phoenix, and many others on the coast of Florida or California, the real estate market is more resilient. It will usually rebound quicker than that of a tertiary market or a rural city, the majority in Oklahoma. Like what happened in Gunnison, the Scottsdale market eventually recovered and revealed an attractive window to sell. Within twenty-four hours of listing the property, I had a purchase contract in hand. Unfortunately, that one fell through. Forty-eight hours after that, I signed another in which the buyer offered us more than our asking price in cash. Ownership traded hands in just a few days' time. Once again, we made a significant profit and unforgettable memories from the investment.

Just before selling the Colorado ranch and the Scottsdale vacation home, we transferred the ownership rights to our commercial real estate company, which allowed us to shield most of the profit from unnecessary taxes. Upon liquidation, we reinvested the proceeds into several strip centers via a 1031 exchange. The high-equity position of our new acquisitions balanced out the company's aggregate debt-to-equity ratio. This concept ties into my Law of Leverage, the core of my real estate philosophy, which I will break down in Chapter Eleven.

Trying to maintain three homes is a challenge. You can only be in one place at a time. Even though you may be able to afford the houses, the situation grows burdensome. As I got older, I desired less complexity in my life. Simplicity will become a craving once you're my age. However, my wife wasn't thrilled about selling either property. She told me to jump in a lake. Instead, I bought us a lake house. She desired a getaway that was closer to Tulsa for the family to share and reconnect, so I followed through when a good deal came around. Our lake house is used much more frequently as it's a manageable one-and-a-half-hour drive away on Grand Lake of the Cherokee, the largest lake in Oklahoma. Years down the line, after we complete our renovations and fill up on the fun, we will secure a hefty profit on this investment during a hot market too.

To be clear, I had no long-term predetermined plan to buy in Scottsdale, Gunnison, or on Grand Lake of the Cherokee. I always kept myself prepared, so when these opportunities arrived at different times in my life, I was able to bridge lucrative investment with leisurely vacations. Again, the key is to diligently save while keeping your eyes open every day to the deals that the market inevitably brings.

Buy a vacation home in the right location. Local supply and demand will dictate your profitability. Buy the property for a conservative price, taking into consideration what the value might be at the end of your hold period. You make your money going in. Finally, enjoy the benefits of the area you settle on and potentially rent it out if you only visit sparingly. Then, once the market swings high, capitalize. Investing can be pleasurable, it just takes some creativity, a lot of discipline, patience, and a bit of earned luck.

BAMBOO INVESTING

Bruce Lee once said, "Notice that the stiffest tree is most easily cracked while the bamboo or willow survives by bending in the wind." Investing with the flexibility of a bamboo will save your financial livelihood. From an investment standpoint, I move in the direction of where the best opportunities are at different points in time. I don't just follow popular trends.

Since the ten years between 1970 and 1980 were dark days to be in the stock market, I shifted my focus elsewhere. When I considered where my money could be best put to use during that time, I concluded that buying farmland was a far more profitable investment. Then, in the early 1980s, tech companies exploded onto the scene. Intel started producing its microchips while Microsoft and Apple released their own versions of the personal computer. This was also around the time when Cerner released its IPO and began selling the software we co-created. There were periods during that technology boom where I made $130,000 in one week, just from the stock market. Making money was a breeze. However, even that growth period hit the brakes by the 1990s, at which point it became tougher to make a substantial return in the technological space for some time. Markets are cyclical by nature. In the back of your mind, you have to be wary of the nosedive. Usually, following such a dramatic period of growth, the stock market will experience a sharp adjustment. This was precisely what followed my success during the boom. Fortunately, by that time I was well diversified.

Some investment vehicles become more appropriate at different times in the evolution of life and business. It's important to constantly review the marginal benefit of each investment. You shouldn't necessarily follow the hype, particularly if it's regarding an investment that has had a long run of success. Eventually, the momentum will fizzle out, which will likely be followed by a period where it will be difficult to make money. In 2021, when interest rates were low, bonds weren't worth investing in. Stocks, on the other hand, looked invincible, and people were dumping money into them like there was no tomorrow. By 2022, we saw a correction that wiped out a lot of short-term day traders, and I-bonds became the new, hot commodity. With the stock market, people think it's always easy to make money because it has historically trended upward in the long term. Although I understand this powerful trend, I have also lived through its limitations in the short term. I don't believe any downturn will last forever, but I've seen one last for a decade! That is a lot of time to wait for a correction. Maybe even too much time, especially for someone nearing retirement or saving up for something like their first house.

If you study wealth generation throughout history, you will find a common pattern: individuals accumulate generous sums of money in multiple different asset classes, as opposed to just one. My experience has been no different. I've developed wealth outside of my medical practice, including from my oil business, art collecting, investments in the stock market, and my real estate holdings, among a few others. There is no single superior asset class throughout time. Some may become obsolete, others timeless, but there will always be a trade-off in dominance. As a result, my exposure to different types of investments has been constantly changing. My portfolio will never stay stagnant.

Investing is fluid, it's flexible, and one rigid strategy will not work in every time period of your life. The most successful investors adapt their strategy to match the hand they are dealt, or what they believe will be dealt to them at any given time. They diversify their portfolio instead of putting all their eggs in one basket. They avoid cracking by bending with the market headwinds.

Focus on keeping your finger on the pulse of the market while continuing to educate yourself on both past and emerging investments on the horizon. Remain open minded and vigilant, understanding where you are in the current market, identifying where the greatest opportunities lie, and then investing in the places that make the most sense as times change. Through this discipline, you'll start to see many more options on the table. This will allow you to be flexible in your investment strategy but firm in your core principles. That is a path to great wealth.

"HOW MANY MILLIONS DID YOU MAKE IN BREEDING AND SHOWING HORSES?"

I t's tough to make money and extremely easy to lose money in the horse business. I consider it more of a hobby than an investment, and a costly one at that. In this business, you've got to love animals and shoveling horse s**t. I figured the two balanced each other out. I started this hobby for the family, and they took it from there. We bred, showed, and even took our pure-bred Morgan horses to competitions. My youngest daughter won four world championships, while my eldest daughter and son each took home a few regional championships. When we travelled out west for national shows, we'd always mix in fun excursions before the event officially started.

The horse business was strictly a labor of love and family passion. Still, to this day, for fun, we take care of a few horses that roam our 100-acre property. Although I didn't make any millions in this business, I was able to reuse the corporation for my oil company which was much more successful. As they say, there's no sense in beating a dead horse.

SEVEN
ROLLER COASTER STOCK MARKET

Side note from Terry:

T he following is non-expert commentary on my part. I'm a medical professional first and foremost. However, I've always been an active investor. I've made some good calls and had some success, but I've also taken losses. On balance I've done reasonably well. The following are my personal observations, lessons learned, and hopefully some helpful words of advice based on my experience in the roller coaster stock market.

MAGIC SPLIT

The stock market can offer magnificent returns, but it's extremely volatile. High risk is built into this platform and unavoidable. Ultimately, that's what investors are rewarded for. It can be a double-edged sword. You'll want to make sure you're on the right part of the blade.

Ironically, the key to maintaining your balance on the knife's edge in this risky arena is to diversify your portfolio across different asset classes outside of the stock market. The best way to do this is by adjusting your allocation of new investable dollars coming in. In practice, I distribute my total investible funds, in varying proportions, to equity investments like real estate or stocks, to debt investments like bonds, and I always retain some degree of more stable liquid investments. The latter category consists of assets that can be easily converted to cash or cash equivalents in a short period of time, like funds held in a money market account.

Even as a single individual, you will have living expenses, insurance, and savings obligations, albeit less than that of someone that is married with greater responsibility. It will serve you well to build up a safety net first, a minimum of six to twelve months of liquid emergency reserves, until you're making enough excess cash to play with riskier investments. This will catch your fall from a lost job, a barren market, or a personal family crisis where you'll need to pull money out fast. To be clear, by "investable funds", I'm referring to the non-crucial income beyond what you need to live. As a young adult limited by the high barrier to entry of big-ticket opportunities like real estate, the stock market might be the only viable option you have. At this stage, consider putting up to 100 percent of your investable funds, that is, any income you rake in beyond the safety net threshold and your regularly reoccurring living expenses, into a stock market index, on which I will elaborate in the next section. Then, as you gain access to other investment opportunities, I recommend periodically readjusting.

Balancing out your investment portfolio by reallocating new dollars coming in looks different as you get older and near retirement. To bring down your exposure to risk from a portfolio that is too stock heavy without cashing out any gains, which would trigger a taxable event, you would instead funnel all the new money you make into short-term bonds, quality bonds, the money market, or other, presumably safer, assets you deem appropriate at that time. A general rule of thumb states that as you near retirement, with each additional investable dollar you earn, you should distribute roughly 40 percent to be held as cash, or a cash equivalent, and invest the remaining 60 percent in riskier assets like stocks, which will be more volatile but will offer higher potential returns. In the past, I've used more robust criteria to distribute my investable funds to market investments. It has led to a proportion that has loosely followed 20 percent to cash or bonds and 80 percent to riskier long-term investments like stocks and real estate. Although I still have significant dollars in the stock market, relative to my overall net worth, it accounts for no more than 10 percent. This proportion continues to drop as I invest more in real estate, which has been my core due to its unique ability to generate consistent cash flow for me. Contrary to popular belief, the specific allocations that make up my healthy portfolio are indicative of opportunity cost, my personal goals, and my life investment horizon, as opposed to rigid percentage guidelines. These considerations have altered the complexion of my portfolio at different times in my life. That's the point.

Opportunity cost is one of the main criteria I use to balance out my portfolio. It's the loss of potential gain from one alternative when another is chosen. Over the last century, from the standpoint of a stock market index that tracks the Standard and Poor's 500 financial benchmark (S&P 500), you can expect to net about a 10 percent average risk-adjusted return each year. The first step I take in analyzing any new investment outside of the stock market is to assess the likelihood of the payoff hurdling this threshold. My money doesn't blindly follow the most popular trends. If I don't believe an alternative investment outside of the stock market will net me at least 10 percent, the deal is auto killed. In other words, if the opportunity cost of placing my capital in the alternative investment, instead of an index that mirrors the S&P 500 benchmark, which has returned investors on average 10 percent over the last hundred-year period, I won't even waste my time. However, if I believe I can exceed that outside of the stock market, then I'm willing to entertain the particular investment further. During the period of stagflation back in the 1970s—something the nation is fast approaching in 2022—I came to the conclusion that the best position I could take was keeping my money out of the stock market altogether and placing it in real estate. I concluded that buying farmland was far more profitable. My portfolio reaped the returns of that allocation. Opportunity cost is checkmark number one. It ensures that my portfolio is effectively growing, working just as hard as I do.

The second consideration relates to my personal goals. When I was fresh out of residency and settling down with my newlywed wife, one of my biggest goals was homeownership. It was something I wanted within one to two years. It was a short-term goal. At the time, I made riskier stock investments that would chase the returns I needed to achieve this goal. I also kept a healthy amount of cash on hand to keep me liquid in case a good deal unexpectedly came about in less than a year. After satisfying the homeownership goal, I set my sights on raising a family. This was a long-term goal that required me to balance my stock investments. I needed to be able to provide for my wife and kids. It made more sense to take a conservative approach to my portfolio so my family would never be left high and dry in a downside scenario. I started looking to safer real estate assets to preserve my wealth and generate cash flow.

Depending on where you are in life, you might be looking to take off on exotic solo trips, raise a family, or start new business ventures. After further refinement of your high-level goals, you might uncover that your primary motivation is either for cash flow, wealth appreciation, or security of income. Your portfolio of investments should always be in alignment with the nature and timeline of your goals to ensure it's working toward getting you what you want when you want it. Exposure to risk is the main lever to play with here. It's imperative you do so in accordance with your life investment horizon.

The final consideration I use to manage my portfolio relates to my life investment horizon. In finance, investment horizon typically refers to the total length of time you expect to hold an investment or security. I'm going to take it one step further. By life investment horizon, I'm referring to the literal amount of lifetime I have left to make up for financial losses in my investment portfolio. As you get older your cushion of protection, of time to ride out down market fluctuations, dwindles. Let's say you are in your sixties preparing to retire, or are newly retired, with a hefty chunk of your portfolio derived from stocks. All of a sudden, COVID-19, an overseas war in Ukraine, or some other dramatic event that you never saw coming, triggers a bear market that sinks your stock savings to the tune of 50 percent over the course of a month. Any return or loss you incur in the stock market is only realized once you sell your position, but given the current economic landscape, and the fact that your income has dried up as you cease to work, you might not have the luxury of passively waiting for your investment to rebound to a profitable state. You might not even have a year to wait. As your life investment horizon dwindled over the past years, you never adjusted your portfolio. Now you're in a race against the clock. That's one you won't want to lose.

A good friend of mine once joked, "I hope the last check I write bounces." He wants to leave nothing behind when he passes on. Obviously, that's an impossible task to time exactly, given that we can't predict our deaths. Most people are happy if they don't run out of money before their last day comes. According to the CDC, the average life expectancy at birth for the total U.S. population was about seventy-eight years in 2022. If you're young, in good physical condition, reasonably healthy, and working, you don't have to be as concerned about your exposure to this timing risk. As you get older, and face an increasingly shorter life investment horizon, you've got to adjust your distribution of assets to cover your rear end. In this situation, it would be wise to start moving to more dependable investments to be assured you'll have the income you need as your timeline shrinks.

When I was young, without much responsibility, I took risks that I wouldn't otherwise repeat at this stage of my life. I recommend investing heavily in the stock market while you're young, partly because your expense load will be lower, especially if you are unmarried, but primarily because it makes more sense for a young person to bet the farm with decades to make up for losses incurred from taking on riskier investments. Young people have time to make a comeback from even the worst-case scenario. But you're not going to be in your twenties forever. The key is to gradually rebalance the complexion of your investment portfolio to hedge against risk. In light of an increasing number of dependents that rely on you or the likelihood of a serious illness as you get older, you will have to do so more aggressively. It should be an ongoing task.

Let me put it like this. When I moved to New York City in my twenties, I was able to fit all my earthly possessions in my small two-door Oldsmobile, and I still had extra room. After I got hitched, had three kids, and moved to Tulsa several years later, I could barely squeeze everything into two moving vans, two flatbeds, and a horse trailer. Your responsibilities and priorities will evolve. Your investment strategy and portfolio should too, which will be largely dictated by opportunity cost, your personal goals, and your life investment horizon. Once you put these three considerations together in action, further insulated by your own unique additions, you will be in congruence with your magic split. This will lead to an optimized risk-adjusted growing portfolio that will allow you to achieve your specific time-bound goals while protecting you from the acute risks that come with age and responsibility.

LESSONS FROM SIXTY YEARS IN THE ROLLER COASTER STOCK MARKET

One. Too many people play the game for short-term profits. Be the long-term player. I generally perceive investing as a lifetime sequence. With some investments, like real estate, even multi-generational.

Trying to time the stock market is like trying to hit a moving target while blindfolded. There will always be ups and downs. Instead of playing the guessing game of when an upswing is going to come and moving your money in and out of the market sporadically, I suggest you invest systematically with the mindset of riding the rollercoaster to the top over time.

Two. As far as investment is concerned, waiting is a great initial policy, at least until you can adequately assess the situation. Individuals make impulsive decisions while reacting to temporary market fluctuations. Be different. When you hear unsettling news or see a drastic change in the economy, sit tight to assess the damage. Don't buy or sell in a reactive way. Wait for the dust to settle, get the facts, and then decide what to do.

Three. Diligently save money while the market is hot. Prepare for the storm while the sun is still shining. When things turn, and they always do, that little bit of preparation will manifest itself in an opportunity for a small number of people to capitalize on extraordinary investments. This was a multi-million-dollar lesson that allowed me to cash in on technology as it was booming in the 1980s. The rest is history.

Four. History gives no exact indication of how a stock will perform in the future. Don't bank on past performance to repeat itself. At the same time, the history of a stock, particularly one with a long-term track record, can reveal useful patterns of how the general population reacts to different economic and social shocks. These insights can help you refine your investment strategy. Although past performance can be a useful consideration, it shouldn't be the sole basis for taking up a position.

HOW I'D PLAY THE GAME

f you think you can consistently time markets, you're fooling yourself. I played that game once upon a time. It didn't end well. I made some gains and lost them just as fast. I suggest riding out the entire market with an index fund. The two main types are mutual funds or exchange-traded funds (ETFs), which are portfolios that match the performance of a specific financial benchmark. One of the most commonly followed financial benchmarks is the S&P 500, which tracks the stock performance of 500 of the largest companies listed on U.S. stock exchanges. To be clear, if a mutual fund and ETF track the same underlying benchmark—if both are tied to the S&P 500 for example—they will perform almost the same. The only difference between the two types is how they are priced and when your order is executed.

The classic approach with a mutual fund is that you place your order, in dollars, during market hours, Monday through Friday. However, the order is only executed at the end of each day. Every twenty-four hours a mutual fund is repriced, except for weekends and holidays. ETFs were created after mutual funds. They are traded in shares, where the price varies throughout the day. You can place an order to buy an ETF at any second while the market is open, and it will execute instantaneously.

For the average investor with a long-term strategy, and especially for a young person, index funds offer a few key benefits. They provide broad market exposure by investing your money in a proportion that ensures the portfolio is well diversified across all sectors and stocks. This makes it possible for you to seize a return on a larger segment of the market, for example 500 stocks across 11 sectors with an S&P-500-based index. They also usually have lower fees because they're automated, regulation-based investments that passively mimic their benchmark. This releases the need for a team of research analysts to constantly monitor and hand pick individual stocks. Lastly, they have low portfolio turnover, meaning they require fewer trades to be placed each year. Fewer trades mean fewer capital gains distributions that incur additional taxes. In other words, an index is a cheap and less risky way to participate in the stock market without extensive research or prior experience.

Investment management companies, specifically stock brokerages, are the platforms that supply mutual funds and ETFs for you to invest in. Some provide stronger foundations than others. My personal favorite is Vanguard, the largest provider of mutual funds and the second-largest provider of ETFs in the world as of January 2021. Vanguard isn't a public company like many other brokerages. It is privately owned by its member funds, which are owned by fund shareholders, rather than by a domineering ownership group. In layman's terms, if you purchase shares of a Vanguard fund, you are a Vanguard owner and retain the power to help shape the company. All the information is online. Be sure to research the unique pros and cons before making your own decision on which investment management company to go with.

Next, in choosing a specific index fund, it's important to consider minimums and expense ratios. Some mutual funds require you to invest a minimum amount to gain access. Many at Vanguard range from $1,000 to $3,000. The first step is to see what you can afford. This is pretty straightforward. What isn't so cut and dry is the expense ratio associated with each fund. The lower the expense ratio the better off you will be, as it's a direct cost that will come out of your pocket as long as you hold the position. These ratios vary, but most should hover around zero.

A few indexes I'd check out are the Wilshire 5000 or VTSAX (Vanguard Total Stock Market Index Fund). It's also possible to buy an ETF made up of the same complexion of stocks. Of course, each brokerage has their unique variation and subset of offerings. As long as you select an index that represents the majority of market gains, your return will align with the above.

Broad market indexes allow you to buy many diverse companies at a lower cost. Large-cap, small-cap, value, and growth stocks will trade off dominance over time. The goal of an index strategy is to diversify, own a pool of the most profitable stocks, and win. Rather than putting all your money in one stock, say Amazon, you hedge your bets and buy into an index that *includes* Amazon, as well as Facebook, Google, and other proven tech giants.

The greatest advantage of these index funds is that they activate upward bias. Conventional wisdom and historical evidence support the observation that on aggregate, stock prices go up over time, driven by inflation and real GDP growth, if nothing else. With market indexes, stocks enter and exit the portfolio all the time. If any one company fails, or if a new more profitable one is created, they can be swapped out. Although indexes can fluctuate in the short term, the investment works to the shareholder's advantage by steadily pushing up the value over the long term. Be patient during the recovery periods so your fund can reach its maximum potential. The gains will eventually average out positively.

Finally, I recommend systematically investing your money using a strategy known as dollar-cost averaging. This is the practice of investing a fixed dollar amount on a regular basis, regardless of the price of the fund. Don't try to time the market, it's a fool's game, just be consistent with an amount you are comfortable with and ride the upward bias over time. Even in the event of a downturn, continue to invest. Doing so will bring down your cost basis which will provide you with grater upside when the market turns. Just don't bother looking at the value of your account. It will be an inaccurate representation of where you will end up long term. Don't worry, a rebound will follow. Stocks are cyclical by nature.

On the other hand, if you receive a large bonus or financial windfall all at once, above and beyond your regular deposit amount, I suggest using a red light, green light investment strategy. This practice involves spreading out new investments over time, which will allow you to adjust to any sudden market swings. For example, if you had $10,000 to dump into an index, you would invest a couple thousand dollars initially and then stop to analyze the market. If you felt it was a wise decision to increase your position, you would spread out the remaining balance over the next two or three quarters. In my investment experience, accumulating several high probability base hits, and occasionally a few doubles, is a much more profitable way to play the game than swinging for the fences every proverbial at bat.

HAND-PICKED

As opposed to passive index funds that mimic the performance of their financial benchmark, actively-managed funds, made up of various hand-picked stocks, aim to *outperform* theirs. For all active managers, including both individuals who actively manage their own money and behemoth firms that actively manage billions of dollars of other people's money, they are rarely able to do so successfully over multiple decades.

If you want to be a successful player of the market, you must become a student of it. That means researching, monitoring, and constantly studying it. It must become the sole focus of your attention. For anyone in a profession outside of Wall Street, that requirement will probably demand more time and energy than they can or are willing to devote. The fact remains, however, that even with extensive experience, 90 percent of active money managers can't consistently beat the financial benchmark they measure against, such as the S&P 500, over the long term. Additionally, because actively-managed funds necessitate many trades, they need to be constantly monitored and, as a result, carry higher expense ratios and fees. The punchline is, before taking your chances with an active approach, either hand-picking individual stocks or hiring someone to do it for you, remember that the market is a tough opponent to beat whether you're an amateur or an expert.

Frankly, I see hand-picking stocks as a form of gambling. With these kinds of investments, I do my homework beforehand, and if I ultimately decide to test my luck on a few individual stocks, I will proceed with the understanding that there is a high probability I could lose all my money. For this reason, I only wager a small amount relative to my total net worth when playing by this strategy. Although picking individual stocks is a risky bet, here are a few fundamentals that have earned me a few bucks over the years:

One. I prefer to invest in long-established companies during temporary shocks in their lifecycle. I try to find great opportunity in bad circumstance. Kraft Heinz was a company that hit some rough waters in 2020 during COVID. A few months after an initial sharp drop, the stock price soared higher than before they ran into any problems. This is just one recent example, but there are an infinite number of similar cases that occur all the time. Track record matters; it's a strong indication of a company's resilience.

Two. Dividend-producing stocks almost always outperform those that don't pay dividends. These are some of the most lucrative stock investments available. In contrast to long-established companies that already pay dividends, recognize that growth-type companies on the upswing are speculative. They lack a proven track record of success and may never make it to a position where an investor will receive a passive dividend. The mortality rate of new companies is quite high. More than half go bankrupt in less than 10 years. The benefit of assuming the extra risk associated with investing in a speculative company is that you're able to buy shares before dividends are issued, usually at a discounted price. If a company does shoot to the moon after you invest, big money can be made. Some great examples of this are companies like Apple and Microsoft. The risk is proportionate to the reward.

Three. I'm an objective investor who sticks to the facts and acts without emotion. To feel comfortable with a company, I can't just rely on my gut feeling. I always research the CEO leading an organization to assess their unique capability. It's important to believe in the captain driving the ship. I also check how much a company is borrowing in comparison to its total assets before investing my hard-earned money. I don't like to see a lot of debt, especially over 50 percent, because it leaves a company with a tiny margin for error. Over-leveraged companies usually find themselves in rough waters sooner or later. Due to their suffocating debt obligations, they are faced with very few options to avoid the wake. That's a sinking ship I don't want to be on.

TO DAY TRADE OR NOT TO DAY TRADE

Day trading is a strategy where an individual buys and sells (or sells and buys) the same security, in this case a stock, on the same day in an attempt to profit from small movements in price. In my opinion, this is a zero-sum game. A smart decision is to avoid day trading. It doesn't make sense to me because no one can forecast the market consistently. It's a proven fact; even the largest firms are struggling. Additionally, markets are driven by computers now, which react quicker than the human mind. This is a significant disadvantage to the individual investor playing the game this way. Day trading is therefore a physically exhausting and expensive strategy that doesn't offer much opportunity to win over the long term.

EIGHT
FINANCIAL BLUEPRINT

"Set a goal of becoming a millionaire for what it will make of you to achieve it. Set a goal that will make you reach. And here's why: the greatest value in life is not what you obtain; the greatest value in life is what you become along the way." – Jim Rohn

"Money is like gasoline during a road trip. You don't want to run out of gas on your trip, but you're not taking a tour of gas stations." – Tim O'Reilly

"Don't judge each day by the harvest you reap, but by the seeds you plant." – Robert Louis Stevenson

VALUE OF MONEY

Money in its physical form is worthless. It can be easily torn apart and carried away with a sudden gust of wind. Yet we all seem to be worried about money to the extent that we don't have it. Given that the bulk of our waking hours are spent accumulating these flimsy green bills, it seems reasonable to understand why we toil so hard for them. How do you value money? Is it a means of acquiring toys and trips? Does it add to your self-worth or feelings of less stress? Does having it allow you to attract more friends, to give more to others, or is it the key to freeing up your time? This seems to be a subjective matter worthy of your attention and deep introspection.

I'm not as rich as Jeff Bezos, but I've had wealth longer than he's been alive. I can tell you, having a bunch of bucks isn't all that exciting. I don't get much satisfaction out of passively counting the zeros in my bank account while the money stagnates. I see money as a tool, a means of reaching a more fulfilling end by what I can do with it, what I become through its pursuit and the experiences I'm afforded along the way. How I'm able to deploy it, to actively put my money to work, makes it vital to me. My answer to the question posed above is this. The money that I make is valuable because it allows me to keep my family and the people that I love secure. My goal has never been to be rich. It has always been for me, and those around me, to be happy. However, security for the family was a large milestone in my pursuit of happiness. It came at a hefty price tag.

When we die, all our assets pass on to the estate. We personally die broke. I have yet to see a U-Haul behind a hearse. This is why I've never been motivated by hoarding a bunch of bucks for myself or buying the newest supercar. Over the years, I've found that money, beyond a certain point, offers diminishing returns. It doesn't offer you much *personally* with regards to a deeper level of satisfaction. It does become endlessly valuable in that it allows you to help other people live better. That creates real substance and an inner feeling that lasts a lifetime. I've been present at the inception and termination of many lives. This is the conclusion I've come to.

One thing to expect when getting into medicine is that you'll meet death. I've stood bedside gripping a patient's hand as I felt the pulse of their heart as they exhaled for the last time. I've also worked in the obstetric service with newborns and started the life of over 150 babies. When you see one person die and another come into existence, you start to form an enlightened view of the circle of life.

Regardless of whether you're worth pennies or millions, you can't stop the clock from winding down. Take it from me, I'm a doctor that fixes clocks for a living. No one can keep them ticking forever. Money is a tool to use, not a reason to live. Keep it in perspective.

FINANCIAL PLAN

O nce you launch your business or begin working for a company on a salary or commission basis, with the money flowing in, what will you do with it? How much will you save and invest? How much will you allocate toward living expenses? Will you need to set something aside for retirement? If you haven't thought through your allocation of money before the capital has settled into your account, you have already forfeited control over your finances. You run the risk of wasting what you worked so hard to make. Before you know it, there's nothing left.

A plan is only a helpful tool so long as it keeps you on the right track, moving toward the specific direction you desire to go. Otherwise, it's just another distraction. Step one is goal setting. Establish what you want at your end destination, or at least at a short-term pit stop along the road. Then back solve from there. More likely than not, your end destination will change as you mature. Your plans will have to evolve as well. Reevaluate them on a quarterly basis to ensure your plan is leading you to a worthy end.

Step two of your financial plan is establishing where you are, meaning listing out your current economic responsibilities. The situation is completely different as you move through the various phases of life, from being single to being in a relationship, and it's a whole new ball game when kids come into play. Where you are will dictate your best course of action moving forward. Be like the good doctor and diagnose before prescribing.

Your financial plan, and more specifically, your budget, is the map, broken down into small actionable milestones, that will keep you inching closer to where you want to be in the most efficient way possible. However, making an effective plan is difficult. It's damn near impossible for anyone lacking industry knowledge and life experience. How can you create an accurate map without a clear vision of the landscape? The good news is that you don't need to have all the answers at once. Through each new experience, and with the newfound knowledge of each successful expert you come across, incorporate your findings into the plan. Keep it flexible, able to evolve over your life.

If your financial plan, or budget, is the road map, then your net worth statement is the unbiased road sign telling you exactly where you are. I recommend that, at the beginning of every year, you get into the habit of penciling one out to see if you've gained any ground over the past twelve months. This practice only gets easier after the first one because it's something you will build off, gradually adjusting a few line items on an annual basis. At the beginning stages of your career, there's going to be a lot of white space on the page. For this reason, it may seem like a waste of time, but this discipline has merit. It'll become an invaluable tool as your portfolio of assets and liabilities grows. It will show you how close you are to achieving your financial goals by keeping track of your actual performance. It's impossible to know who's winning the game if no one's keeping score.

On January 1, when things calm down after the holidays, many people, myself included, do a net worth while watching the college football bowl games. Since I personally guarantee some of the loans for my real estate company, the bank requires me to update my net worth annually in order for them to reassess my creditworthiness. Even if it wasn't mandatory, I would still elect to do one. Putting my first few together revealed all my debt free assets when I was younger. It was a true revelation that released a lot of unnecessary stress. It validated that my hard work and budget were paying off. A net worth statement can also be a much-needed kick in the ass if you're behind schedule. The numbers never lie. Getting that kick in the rear end at least once a year should be sufficient to keep you on pace to achieving financial freedom.

THE ROAD TO FINANCIAL FREEDOM

F inancial freedom is being able to choose how to spend your time without the constraints of your personal finances. If your goal is to be financially free, spending money is not always the problem and saving money alone is not always sufficient to get you there. It's a matter of both *disciplined* spending and *diligent* saving.

As a child, I didn't get everything I wanted, but my sister and I always had what we needed because our parents spent money wisely. I learned that even though you may be able to afford various things throughout your life, you have to consider whether you are spending on a need or a want. Furthermore, you must think through the expected upside from each dollar spent. If your finances are tight, my advice is to start by prioritizing the needs. As your money grows, it's okay to spend on some of the wants for your own pleasure. However, no matter what your bank account looks like, always stay true to yourself, not to an image painted by the trendiest blogger. I cemented this key principle into my young philosophy, and no amount of money has ever been able to change it.

George Kaiser is a fellow Tulsa native who inherited a struggling oil company in the 1960s and led it back to profitability in a dramatic 180-degree turnaround. A few decades later, during the financial downturn of the 1980s, he bought Bank of Oklahoma in a fire sale as it was on the verge of bankruptcy. Once again, he transformed it into a lucrative institution across multiple states. Kaiser became a multi-billionaire for his efforts.

What most people don't know is that Kaiser had humble beginnings. I believe that during his upbringing, he too developed principles, values, and beliefs that became a part of his psyche before he ever made his first million. Now in old age, he is said to prefer commercial flights over charter and to own no private yachts. Is this because he dislikes recreation and luxury? Unlikely. I believe it's because he has no one to impress. He's playing by his rules. I think he derives deeper satisfaction from spending his wealth through the three-billion-dollar foundation he established, which distributes more than $40 million a year to revitalize his native city. Kaiser made a public commitment to give away his fortune to the community. In the past, he's offered $10,000 to any working-class adult who moved to Tulsa. Most notably, in 2018, his foundation opened "Gathering Place", one of the largest public parks ever built with private funds, spanning over sixty-six acres, to the tune of $465 million. There is no entrance fee, and the foundation maintains the entire park. It's a unique attraction for friends and family to connect without an electric outlet in sight.

Kaiser is continuing to splurge on what gives him the greatest return, even if that return is only emotional. Does it surprise you that he contributes the bulk of his time and money to the buckets of philanthropy, business, and family, rather than buying the shiniest new toys even though he can afford all of them? It doesn't surprise me. Living by the principle of staying true to himself, which helped earn his abundant wealth in the first place, was a nonnegotiable part of his philosophy that he was never willing to budge on. He stuck to the fundamentals that led to his phenomenal success. Now, I'm not an advocate of giving away all your money, although I firmly believe in the emotional return you'll receive by giving away some. I also enjoy luxury just as much as the next person. I never had a supercar in the driveway, but I do sport a Lexus, which is a high-quality, functional vehicle that drives smooth as butter. The point is, play by your own inner scorecard. Spend according to your personal hierarchy of values, not on what might boost your image in the eyes of others. Spending to satisfy external motivations will likely break your bank account, but more importantly, it will break your spirit.

For the next month, track every single thing you spend on, including your overall net cash flow at month's end, in an Excel workbook or on paper. If you aren't managing your expenses, your expenses are managing you. This simple exercise will open your eyes to the stark reality that many of your purchases return a relatively small amount of long-term satisfaction and a lot of short-term pleasure. If over 90 percent of what you spend is funneled into clothes, burritos, and rent payments, you may want to scratch your head and consider what your life is going to look like continuing on the current trajectory. To change course altogether, you might pick up the habit of weighing the *value* and *utility* you are set to gain from each item or experience before swiping your card. Siphoning potential purchases through this filter will manifest in a very different dollar figure on the next month's income statement. It might even put a smile on your face.

Let me clarify: eliminating all your expenses is not the goal. Hoarding mounds of green paper under your mattress over a lifetime will only give you an increasingly lumpy sleep. You won't receive much value or utility from that. What matters most is having the discipline to spend what you diligently save on the right products, investments, and lifestyle.

A large income doesn't equate to financial freedom. Consider the lawyer with a $300,000 salary who only saves 10 percent of it after paying down debt, tax, luxury bar tabs, and other frivolous lifestyle expenses. You would have more money in your pocket earning $70,000 a year as an entry-level analyst and saving half of it. It doesn't take a huge paycheck to live free, it takes wise asset management. In other words, it's not about how much you make but how much you keep.

If you're not managing your expenses, you can't save. If you can't save, you'll have nothing to invest. What will result is a grim cycle where you break your back through the day, waste all you make, and by the time you hang your hat at nightfall, you will have no choice but to reset your alarm for dawn and pound the pavement again. This sinister merry-go-round commands your most valuable asset, time. It's a ride that will leave you with a throbbing headache.

Financial freedom is, more specifically, freedom of choice, as it relates to how you can afford to spend your time. One of the greatest benefits my financial philosophy has been the ability to pursue my truest passions through a meaningful career while being able to maintain an exhilarating lifestyle surrounded by family and friends. It has never been about owning the newest Ferrari or boasting the largest bank account. Spending a week cruising on the boat at our family's lake house, while my screaming grandkids smash through the wake on a pair of Sea-Doos, without having to worry about losing my job, or safely enjoying a midweek glass of vintage wine with my wife and close friends on our ranch, without interruption, have been the most rewarding treasures of financial freedom. None of this was by accident. It was a matter of disciplined spending and diligent saving. It was saving money consistently each day so that I could continuously invest in opportunities that would return me a greater amount than I put in. Because of this consistent hard work, I've been able to spend my time on my own terms. I wish the same for you.

VELOCITY

The velocity of money is the rate at which consumers and businesses in an economy collectively spend money. A high velocity is usually associated with a healthy, expanding economy. The faster you place your capital in higher-interest-bearing environments, the healthier your own personal finance economy will be. Keep your investable dollars working for you all the time by swiftly transferring them out of a bank account.

You have to keep a certain amount of money in your bank account to be able to issue checks and pay short-term liabilities. However, I wouldn't leave any excess beyond that stagnating for long, because you will either receive minimal interest or none at all. I usually sweep all of my investable income, beyond my monthly living expenses, at a high velocity, into a Vanguard municipal money market fund. I'll keep the money there in the meantime while I search for an opportunity that will amplify my return based on my needs at that time.

Hastily transferring your money out of a bank account can also be a safer strategy as I've personally witnessed banks go bust. I can vividly remember one summer some years back when this became a frightful reality for me. A bank not too far from my medical center went bankrupt, and the Feds rushed in to take the reins of its operations. After I finished the day's work, my son and I decided to see the events unfold for ourselves. We weren't allowed into the bank, but we watched as a plethora of federal government auditors flooded the building. A dizzying number of account holders subsequently lost money. I told myself that this was a vision I should never forget. Maintain a healthy personal economy by quickly moving your money out of a bank's tight grip.

THE SAVING SPECTRUM

The best place to park your money should align with what you want and when you want it. If you're saving for something short term, keep your money somewhere stable and liquid so you'll have immediate access to it, even if you have to sacrifice some upside to avoid excessive volatility. For example, early in your career when you aren't making it rain, maxing out long-term retirement accounts could lock up your cash and eliminate flexibility, which would be detrimental to your goal of buying a house if that is an aspiration you have in the near future. It would also be unwise to store your money in the stock market, aside from some conservative mutual index funds or ETF index funds, if you're planning to pull it out in less than a year or two. The market is unpredictable. It could fluctuate, leaving you in a jam right when you need your money most. In this case, keeping your savings in the money market is probably the best option. The single-digit percent return isn't much gain, but the benefit is the ability to pull the money out quickly and safely. The purpose of this short-term savings strategy is not to make you rich. It's meant to keep your money readily available, at or slightly above its value, so you will be able to act on an opportunity where real money or value can be gained.

The goal of long-term saving is to grow the money that you don't immediately need. It's meant to generate returns that you'll be able to live off once you retire. The strategy of parking money for the long term may include real estate holdings, stock indexes, or retirement accounts. Two of the most common types of retirement accounts are Roth IRAs and 401(k) plans, which differ in two main ways as it relates to taxation. Obviously, this is subject to change over the years. With the Roth IRA, you pay taxes when you contribute to your account. Alternatively, 401(k) contributions are pre-taxed, which means your money is taxed when you pull it out of the account upon retirement. Each retirement plan has its own strategic advantages.

With the amount of money that the government is currently borrowing, it's reasonable to assume Congress will set higher tax rates in the future to pay back the nation's astronomical debt load. If you believe that rate hikes are on the road ahead, waiting to pay your taxes in the future could be more costly. Additionally, given that your account balance will only grow over the years, it's most advantageous to contribute to a Roth IRA as early as possible, starting in college if you have extra cash on hand. Essentially, you'll be paying a lower tax rate on a smaller sum of money. The returns that compound over your life will not be taxed when you pull them out decades later, ideally at a hefty profit. However, Roth IRAs have a maximum contribution limit on the amount that can be deposited each year as well as participation restrictions based on your level of income. Another distinction is that, unlike the Roth IRA, 401(k) plans have required minimum distributions, or "RMD" rules. This means that, at a certain point in your senior years, your account will automatically disperse cash whether you need the funds or not. This will create new and potentially unwanted taxable income. It's also possible to do a combination of both a Roth IRA and a 401(k) plan. Many companies will sponsor their own versions for their employees. Some will even offer to match your contributions. Consider taking full advantage if that option is on the table. Do your research ahead of time and then take a calculated risk based on your personal goals.

THE POWER OF PENSIONS

Pension programs function like 401(k) plans. You can deposit pre-taxed income, however, when you pull out your money down the road, you must pay the current tax rate on the entire sum at that time. Pensions are also made up of funds you're not going to touch until retirement. There is a caveat though. You can pull your money out prematurely, but you will have to pay taxes on it and usually an additional penalty. You can also borrow a certain amount of money from your pension program, but only if you pay yourself back with reasonable interest. I've never done that, but I've seen people do so in pressuring situations. Some of these individuals later ran into problems refilling the account, which put their entire pension in jeopardy.

Pension funds diversify your money across different investments. Stock market indexes are commonly used here because the upward bias complements the long-term nature of the program. It's also possible to buy real estate through your pension, and I've done this twice.

There have been some situations where I've left my investments in place for a significant length of time, which has usually been the case with my personal taxable accounts, but there have also been other situations where I've been in the market through my pension program and have shifted around my investments more frequently. I can afford to be flexible with my pension investments because I'm not affected by the same tax consequences for doing so, as long as I don't cash any money out of the account. I routinely adjust the complexion of my overall portfolio by rebalancing the assets in my pension program. This is an effective way to hedge your exposure to risk without triggering a taxable event.

Upon joining St. John Health System in Tulsa, all of us doctors were using different banks to oversee each of our individual pension plans. We were all paying exorbitant expense ratios. Around the 1980s, Health Maintenance Organizations, or HMOs, shook up the medical industry. These groups provided health insurance plans that limited coverage to care only from doctors who worked for or contracted with them. HMOs had all the leverage because they funneled such a large amount of business to the doctors in their network. As a result, HMOs only paid a capitated flat rate on behalf of their members, which shifted the risk back onto the doctors, who had to provide treatment for these patients within the budget of funds they received. HMOs limited a doctor's ability to mark up prices, which allowed them to keep the cost of their health insurance plans low. This structure resonated with me. I thought applying it to our finances would make a lot of sense too. A lightbulb went off in my head. "Why don't all of us doctors pool our money together and direct our pensions to one provider of management services, which will give us leverage to renegotiate our outrageous individual costs?" The idea was to grow the aggregate value of our plans to a size that would incentivize one money manager to trend their expense ratio downward for all of us if they wanted to keep our business. At the birth of our combined pension fund, I figured that we'd be extremely lucky to get a total contribution of $3 million. My expectations were shattered; the plan swelled to $20 million right off the bat. As more doctors joined the program, we added all their employees too. The web spread out even further. As it grew, our collective financial position kept improving.

Initially we used a few different Wall Street investment firms to manage our money. We subsequently created a steering committee of doctors to meet with them at least once a year to break down their performance. Over time, we figured out where they were making a killing. This was mainly through taking a percentage of the investable funds in our account, but they may have also profited off the spread between the bid and ask price in each trade we made. I disliked how, even if they had a poor year where our members didn't earn much of anything, these managers still got their hefty cut off the top. Back then, it wasn't unusual for that cut to hover around 5 percent of total assets under management. There was also another standard option at that time to instead structure a manager's compensation as a larger portion of just the gains they made for us that year. If our plate was empty, they wouldn't eat. In the event of a strong year, their fee had the potential to morph into a monstrous dollar figure.

Money managers who invest in anything other than small caps can't really add a lot of value, so we no longer use them. We only contract with an institutional bank, for a relatively low fee, to handle the legal requirements and government documents that must be filed correctly. Currently, our pension plan is heavily involved in mutual index funds and ETFs, which allow our participants to capture the gains of the overall stock market inexpensively. We recommend a tailored portfolio to each member, dependent on their age and risk preference, with strategies ranging from conservative to aggressive. Each individual's contribution is then distributed in accordance to their personalized strategy, on a periodic basis, until their allocation goals are met. Their long-term investment is put into overdrive, fully automated, so each participant can focus all their time and energy on just being a doctor, which is why the plan has been so successful.

The original pension fund we began in the 1980s is currently running at around $350 million today. It has been life changing for many of our members who have had the security to retire sooner due to the preservation and growth of pre-taxed income that they worked so hard to make over their career. This should be the goal of your own pension plan.

MOMENTUM

With the ability to finance a real estate deal in numerous ways, and in the current environment of skyrocketing rental rates, property ownership is an amazing opportunity to pursue, both financially and emotionally. This phenomenon goes beyond the primal necessity for shelter. It will give you confidence early in life that is hard matched. It's a true form of momentum. I became a homeowner in an unconventional way. Although it was far from my dream home, it was my start.

Throughout medical school and my time in the U.S. Public Health Service, I diligently saved. I was young, so I didn't have much in the way of expenses, and I was disciplined with my finances. My newlywed wife, Mary Beth, was on the same page. By the time we moved to Rochester, Minnesota, for my residency at the Mayo Clinic, our ownership journey began in the form of a somewhat cramped two-bedroom home in a tiny subdivision of other tightly-built homes. Let's call it functional. It was the polar opposite of modern, developed during World War II for returning servicemen. We assumed a thirty-year government mortgage at a 4 percent interest rate, which was cheap at that time, and then we paid the difference in cash up front.

Over the years, this note had been assumed by other young doctors, like me, who just needed a place to stay during their training. Due to the nature of these temporary living situations, none of the previous owners had put much equity into the property. In other words, this house had been flipped multiple times at a break-even price. Regardless of its unusual backstory, this house checked three boxes that made it a success for my wife and me. First, it was inexpensive and didn't break our bank accounts. Second, it gave us shelter. Third, and perhaps most importantly, it made us homeowners. That old bunker was a win. In my experience, your first home will likely be the hardest one to get, it may even be the ugliest, but it does get easier, and better, after that. Resilience to stay in the game will be your weapon of choice.

Upon the completion of my training at the Mayo Clinic, I was brought on as a full-time staff member. My wife and I decided to cash in on a four-acre property in the country, outside Rochester, in a quiet little town coincidentally called Mayo Wood. We lived there until I accepted my role at MAWD Pathology Group, in Kansas City, at which point we switched things up and purchased a newer home that was under construction in the suburbs. It seemed only fitting since we had kids by then. We quickly discovered our dislike for densely-populated neighborhoods after living without neighbors for so long. However, we did like the development aspect of this experience, especially being able to personalize the home to fit our needs. We then started hunting for an open plot of land outside the city.

This was around the time I became familiar with the local farmer I mentioned in Chapter Six who owned thirty-five acres of farmland in the green plains of Smithville, Missouri. He was interested in selling his property to fund his looming retirement, so we agreed on seller financing. Our family built a new house on the land and continued to scale up from there. By the time we moved down to the Sooner State, we had saved up enough money to buy land and build our dream home, with all cash, here in Tulsa.

Some of the most satisfying wins in my life came unexpectedly. Instead of trying to play the guessing game of when an opportunity would come, I chose to focus each day on growing my capability. To better position myself for home ownership, I improved my problem-solving skills, educated myself on the fundamentals of real estate, and worked hard in my career so I could save and invest. There was no secret to it; I just mastered the part of the process that was in my control. Your own story will likely play out differently, but I believe it will be just as exhilarating.

PART FOUR

BUILDING A REAL ESTATE DYNASTY

Disclaimer from the author:

This part of the book explains how a man without any real experience in commercial real estate or professional connections was able to identify, acquire, and profit off investment properties for over two decades while working full time in the field of medicine. Obviously, this is a framework that worked for Terry. Your market and financial situation may look different. The thought process behind why he does what he does and the principles that dictate his actions in real estate are the keys to replicating his success. His mindset, shaped by over twenty years of real estate ownership, is the golden egg. It has been cracked open for you in the following chapters.

NINE
BREAKING ONTO THE SCENE

Note from the author:

Arnold Schwarzenegger, the world famous Austrian American with bulging muscles, one of the most prolific bodybuilders ever to lift in the sweaty air of a gym or to walk the set of a highly-esteemed action-packed Hollywood thriller, became a millionaire buying commercial real estate in the 1980s before his movie career took off. This is another example of how an individual that started out from humble beginnings with a primary occupation outside of real estate broke onto the scene and generated wealth through this lucrative investment. Schwarzenegger describes his early mindset in an interview on *The Tim Ferriss Show*:

> I feel like if I am smart with real estate and take my little amount of money that I make in bodybuilding, and in seminars, and in selling my courses through mail orders, I could save enough to put down money for an apartment building. I realized in the 1970s that the inflation rate was very high and therefore an investment like that was unbeatable. Buildings that I would buy for 500K within the year were 800K and I put only maybe 100K down, so you made 300 percent on your money. You couldn't beat that. I quickly developed and traded up more apartment and office buildings on Main Street down in Santa Monica.

OUTSIDER

Dr. Terrence Dolan: Once I decided it was time to sell the oil company and exchange the proceeds for commercial real estate, in the early 2000s, I started scouring all the properties coming to market. I quickly became aware of what was transacting and educated myself on the fundamentals of the various product types available. It quickly dawned on me that a relatively small number of brokers represented most of the public listings in my market. Just scroll through the inventory of an online database like CoStar or take a short drive around your local shopping center, and you'll likely see the same few names on the marketing collateral and large "For Sale" or "For Lease" signs fronting the buildings. As far as properties I was interested in, they were few and far between. One could say I was searching for a unicorn. Eventually I figured out that almost all the high-quality deals were never publicized. They were bought, usually off market, by a consortium of brokers and their private investor cronies. I never even had a chance to compete. It was a hard pill to swallow as an investor looking to break onto the scene, but I knew I had to suck it up and adjust my strategy if I was going to overcome this unexpected barrier to entry.

As a pathologist in laboratory medicine, I wasn't on a first-name basis with many brokers; in fact, I rarely came across any in my line of work. I was an outsider. Subsequently, my new business was stagnating. It took me a while to start making connections to the movers and shakers in the area. I knew that if I had any hope of finding my unicorn, the best course of action was to cultivate close relationships with these elite brokers and diligently follow up. This wasn't going to happen overnight, but I've always been a long-term player, so it was a game I knew I could win. I strapped in for the ride. At the beginning of your own real estate journey, keep your finger on the pulse of the market, and, eventually, you'll form a deeper understanding of the key players in your geographic area. Once you tap into these expert resources, you will have a higher success rate in identifying and acquiring strong deals. It will simply be a matter of time.

My first opportunity to buy a premium property came unexpectedly. I always kept myself in a position to execute. Leading up to acquisition number one, I was looking without really knowing what the hell I was doing. After speaking with a handful of mid-level brokers, I was directed to a well-respected veteran broker named Paul Williams. Williams was originally an attorney who had switched careers. During the recession of the 1980s, he was involved in overseeing many bankruptcy transactions and was able to pass on some lucrative opportunities to his rolodex of investors. He filled his own pockets in the process. I made contact via an old-fashioned cold call. It didn't take long to recognize how well established he was. This was the type of individual I was willing to trust. He boasted a powerful reputation and a proven track record backed by successful experience. I revealed to him that I was looking to sell my oil production company to buy commercial real estate. Oklahoma law considered the land associated with my oil leases real estate assets, which allowed me to execute a 1031 exchange and avoid paying capital gains taxes by rolling all the proceeds directly into another property. I explained that I had already found a buyer for the oil company, but that I was in desperate need of an up leg—in other words, a replacement property—to purchase immediately. I needed his help, and I was on the clock to close due to the timing rules of the 1031.

Williams and I had a mutually beneficial relationship. When his wife and child ran into medical complications, I helped his family gain access to the Mayo Clinic. In a similar way, he connected me with the best deals that came across his desk. Add value to others first and your return will follow.

In business, I've found that the way you treat people matters. By projecting an honest and knowledgeable presentation of your character in all your dealings, you will gradually gain the trust of the professionals around you, even the ones you don't know. Not only will they be motivated to help you achieve *your* goals, they will also reach out when *they* need guidance in your area of expertise, allowing you to return the favor. This reciprocal principle works whether you are an engineer, lawyer, doctor, or computer technician, looking for help in breaking onto the scene in another field. When starting something new, you can't overcome every obstacle on your own. You will need allies. However, unlike in a war, where the largest army usually wins, in the real estate business you don't necessarily need the greatest number of connections. What you do need are a few extraordinary connections, what I call "champions". Paul Williams was one of my champions in commercial real estate.

Our initial conversation changed everything. Over the next month he informed me whenever he heard about a property that fit my clearly defined criteria. Usually these were the elusive off-market deals I had struggled to find earlier. One of the deals he sent me was an interesting retail property on South Peoria Avenue in an evolving neighborhood in southwest Tulsa. The location was superb, the numbers penciled, and retail was one of the strongest performing products at the time. He helped me negotiate and close the deal, and I subsequently hired his firm to manage the property for the first year so my team could learn how to manage it in the long term. We bought the property fully occupied. By the end of the year, all our tenants had stayed. A couple years down the line we did run into some turnover, but by that point we had enough knowledge and experience to overcome the issue. Our South Peoria center has increased in value from what we originally bought it for, around $1.1 million, to $2.8 million the last time we had it appraised. Along with value appreciation, we have received positive cash flow and depreciation benefits every single year that we've owned it.

When the market was hot, I couldn't find anything worthwhile. As I became better connected to the local specialists, the buried treasures revealed themselves. To this day, I try to answer every cold call I receive from real estate brokers, young or old. I deflect their offers to sell, but I'm polite and explain to them exactly what I'm interested in buying. If you're detailed in your criteria, you will come first to mind, or even better, to the top of their call list, when they uncover a property that fits the description. This will save you time sifting through unactionable deals that don't align with your investment goals. Let the brokers do the heavy lifting for you. It's their job.

Commercial real estate is a relationships game. Success is a matter of becoming an insider. As you make connections, it's important to display your proficiency in solving problems, your in-depth knowledge of the business, or willingness to learn the business, and to establish yourself as a long-term player, not just another shooting star in the night. As we continued to expand our business, we became a household name on the local brokers' periodical list of closings. The more credibility we got with the top movers and shakers, the more leads they shot our way. They recognized we would likely become repeat clients. Dollar signs formed in their eyes. Of course, a broker is not the only means of finding a lucrative property. It just made the most sense in my situation since I was working full time in a completely different profession without many connections.

I didn't know a tremendous amount about the industry when I started. I was fluent in business, comfortable with diving into new experiences, and willing to search for the answers I lacked. We all have the unique opportunity to learn something new each day, but we must be humble enough to play the role of the student and put in the effort to build on our existing knowledge. Doing so allowed me to construct a dynasty from nothing.

Like your first home, acquiring your first investment property is going to be the hardest one to get, especially as an outsider. This goes for many things in life when you lack experience and relationships. Your first $100,000 will be the toughest to make, your first race will be the most difficult, and your first real job will likely be the biggest struggle. Don't get discouraged; everything is easier the second time around. Refrain from letting your emotions dictate your decision-making process when times get tough, and be patient, realizing that it takes time to come across an accretive deal. Use your discipline to walk away from the bad properties, and when you stumble upon one that's worth it, move quickly and decisively to break onto the scene.

FROM GROUND ZERO

O ur team learned a lot from the failures and successes of our first retail property. We wanted more but couldn't find enough quality deals. It took a lot of discipline to pass up on the mediocre properties and wait for the ones that mirrored our business model to come along. The good news was that we were on a first-name basis with many more key players compared to our first go-around.

I kept in contact with Paul Williams. Shortly after closing on Peoria Avenue, he alerted me that two buildings on Yale Street, in the middle of downtown Tulsa, were likely to trade soon. The property was owned by a group of retired neurosurgeons. The younger partners in the group didn't want to invest in the buildings anymore. The philosophical difference had caused friction between the old dogs and new pups. This was a dynamic I knew all too well. I stayed in the background, a fly on the wall, with a low-ball offer that I stuck to. Eventually they accepted it. I diagnosed this as a classic case of medical professionals acting as lackluster businessmen. These properties were in high demand, directly adjacent to St. Francis Hospital, the predominant healthcare system in the state of Oklahoma, and we paid them off fast.

Not long after that purchase, a portfolio of Blockbuster video stores came to market. Two of them aligned with our company's real estate philosophy, so we pulled the trigger. One is in Claremore, northeast of Tulsa, and one is in Sand Springs, a bedroom community about ten minutes west of Tulsa. Of course, over the next five years Blockbuster went bust. For an owner who had purchased one of the properties in a less desirable location or overpaid altogether, this would've pulled the curtains on their investment. I always took calculated risks, meaning I considered contingencies ahead of time. Before I signed a purchase agreement, I would run through a stress scenario, assuming all the current tenants were to depart. Quality of location is the main variable that determines how fast a building will fill back up again. The desirability of the area was what I ultimately hung my hat on. Sure enough, when Blockbuster exited stage left, we redeployed the assets immediately. It didn't take long to find new tenants. Both properties have been fully occupied since. Buying at the right price in a great location will make or break your real estate career. Never split the difference on this.

The last project that got our real estate company off the ground came in the form of an entitled piece of land in Sand Springs owned by a developer who had recently completed building a Walmart adjacent to the site. After completion of the main building, he was motivated to sell the residual pieces of land to cover the interest payments on his loan. We paid a premium price for our asset, but it was in a location we desperately wanted. When we first bought in Sand Springs, there wasn't much in the way of competition among businesses because it was considered somewhat of a backward community. Now it has totally come of age. It's quite aggressive in attracting tenants, especially with Walmart driving foot traffic to the submarket. A large part of assessing a location is foresight, anticipating what the potential landscape will look like five to ten years out. Our estimates proved to be correct.

Shortly after this acquisition, something unexpected happened. We found out that an auto mechanic had previously closed on the land adjoining our new property with the intention of building a vehicle repair shop. At the time, he was running his business out of another location across town. I spoke with the broker who sold the parcel to him and mentioned, "If he changes his mind, here's my number." As they often do, the mechanic's plans fell through. In the coming weeks our team took the problem off his hands. We built a strip center across both plots of land.

I had no idea that my real estate journey was going to play out as it did. I kept myself educated and never deviated from my core investment principles. That's the beauty of this game; anyone can play if they're willing to learn. Our team figured out the nuances as we went, erring on the conservative side as we maneuvered through new terrain. Knock on wood, to this day we haven't made any major mistakes. That's not to say we haven't had any minor slip-ups, but we were able to catch our balance and derive valuable lessons through the shaky process. These lessons ultimately facilitated our lasting success.

An example of the above is how we paid up for some early properties, meaning we thought we slightly overpaid for a few assets *at the time*. As the population and surrounding market developed, these properties turned out to be some of our top performers, commanding higher rents each year. This was the case with our strip center situated right off a main throughfare, on Memorial Street, which slices through the middle of Tulsa. When we first analyzed this deal, the only thing around the property was overgrown weeds. However, we believed there was a high probability that the area would be completely readapted, as it was situated in the center of the city. This speculation was also shared by the seller, an insurance broker who had a passion for making money. Fortunately, we were able to negotiate a deal to buy him out. During the first few years, while there wasn't much going on around us, it was a tough center to lease out. Just as we were about to write off the project as a loser, the population boomed. Since then, another large Walmart set up shop adjacent to us along with several new developments, which have collectively flipped the local market on its head. Ironically, today to an outsider lacking perspective, it would seem that we bought the Memorial Street center for a monstrous discount. This lesson reiterates just how important it is to anticipate the evolution of a location.

THE GRAY SHEEP

I f I had to point to a property that was the biggest challenge for us, without hesitation, it would be a strip center we developed in Sand Springs. It wasn't quite the black sheep of our portfolio, but it definitely fell into the gray area. The issue stemmed from buying a property with poor street visibility in a location that had weak population demographics.

A short while after we bought one of the Blockbusters I mentioned previously, which was on a hard corner in Sand Springs, an old Mobil station came to market directly adjacent to it. Having two parcels in such close proximity allows you to have greater pricing power in the local market as it pertains to rents. It also activates economies of scale, which decreases management costs. It seemed to be a great deal. There was just one glaring problem. Off the backside of our Blockbuster, which was on a busy thoroughfare, there was a steep drop off, which killed the new property's street visibility. For retail tenants who wanted their businesses to be in clear sight of drive-by customers, this sloping hill was a huge turnoff. We knew the project was going to take some work, but nothing out of the ordinary, or so we thought.

The seller was an elderly woman who was motivated to cash out. We approached her and negotiated a fair price reflective of the location, which was just decent. Once the property was tied up, we flattened the existing gas station and planned a small strip center development on the parcel. That's when the problems started. We had to bring in dirt to raise the future building up, and after that we dealt with new drainage issues. That was just the beginning.

Upon finishing construction, we were able to lease out the end caps very quickly. The rest of the space sat vacant for a while. We eventually figured out that, due to the lack of street visibility, the space was more suitable for an office tenant mix than it was for retail shops. Since then, we have leased out most of the remaining square footage to tenants like an accounting group, a public insurance broker, and a healthcare company. It was like a puzzle trying to piece together how to market this property. Once we finally addressed the root problem, the pieces fell into place synergistically. We never lost money. The property has seen positive cash flow. However, it didn't achieve the same returns as our other centers. Still, demand for the location continues to improve as the population expands, and our rate keeps getting better on each newly signed lease.

This strip center was a challenge from the start. Our saving grace was that we bought it inexpensively, so our cost basis was always manageable. Additionally, we paid all cash, so we never had to worry about a debt obligation from a bank. This generous safety margin was intentional. It allowed us to wait for the right kind of tenants who would pay top dollar. We never had to settle for absurd discounts.

We overcame our struggles with unforgettable lessons that, for better or for worse, we had to learn the hard way. Regardless of how intense the desire is, never overpay for a property, but realize that paying a premium for a location that has future promise can often become the greatest discount. Understand that your safety margin is dictated by how you finance the asset, which, in our case, was coming out of pocket with all the cash. This saved us during periods of low occupancy and cash flow. Finally, be creative in how you market your property to attract new tenants when things go sideways. Hopefully you can learn from our gray sheep so all your opportunities turn into unicorns.

"DO YOU CONSIDER YOUR REAL ESTATE COMPANY A SUCCESS?"

I n the early 1980s, while my son toiled alongside me in our oil company, he enjoyed the accounting work he was doing, but he grew to despise the inherent turbulence of the industry. As a result, in the early 2000s, when oil prices finally ascended from the depths, we strategically made our exit. My son was far more optimistic about real estate, where the dramatic and unpredictable volatility seemed to evaporate altogether. A lot of his stress evaporated too. I built the real estate company primarily to give our family something to grow together.

When we acquired our first property, my eldest daughter took the reins with my son and me. My youngest daughter was living 700 miles away in Colorado Springs. I always desired to bring our entire family back together in Tulsa, but I needed a compelling reason for my youngest to even consider the move. Offering her the opportunity to co-run our company was the answer.

Despite all the uncertainty and novel challenges they've faced, my three children have facilitated the growth of our company. My oldest daughter later parted ways to pave her own real estate path, and I'm proud of her for making the move. The last thing I would have wanted was for her to pursue something she lacked a burning passion for. As it turns out, my other children complement each other quite well in their respective duties. My son plays the heavily numerical role of accounting and tracking the numbers. He maintains the relationship to the broker community and is a licensed real estate broker in the state of Oklahoma. Meanwhile, my youngest daughter is the personal relationship individual, acting as the face of the business, visiting with the lessees, and dealing with acute issues at any particular center. She maintains the relationship with our tenants and is a licensed real estate agent in the state of Oklahoma. All other jobs are contracted out or shared between them, and big decisions are mulled over by the three of us collectively.

I started the company because I wanted to bring my family together. It wasn't solely for investment purposes. Of course, we are thrilled with the income our real estate investment has produced, but we have benefited far more from what it's done to unite the family. In this sense, I consider the real estate company one of my greatest successes.

TEN
THE ART OF ACQUIRING

Side note from Terry:

've anchored all my properties in Tulsa due to the nature of my career, family interests, and lifestyle preferences. The Coast Guard taught me that an anchor keeps the ship steady. Be that as it may, these fundamental principles can certainly be applied to any other primary, secondary, or tertiary market between New York and San Diego. Although some of the nuances of your strategy will need to be tweaked based on population density, surplus of open land, and local supply and demand characteristics, the principles in this chapter are universal by nature. This approach to real estate can work on Sixty-Eighth Street in Manhattan or Old Town Road. One thing is for sure, if these conservative principles can work in Tulsa, they can work anywhere.

MOTIVE

Why does anyone purchase investment real estate, properties they aren't going to live in? It boils down to three main motivations: security of income, cash flow, and wealth preservation and appreciation. My primary focus is cash flow.

Our company's real estate strategy is to buy value-add properties that we can either physically improve through construction or operationally improve through our management component to generate consistent cash flow in the long term. These assets must be in easily accessible locations with strong population demographics and able to be bought at reasonable prices, with our sweet spot sitting between $1 million and $4 million. Of course, these opportunities are hard to come by. When one does appear, we know that there are many other like-minded investors frothing at the mouth. It can be a dog fight.

We walk away from most of the properties we evaluate since getting ahold of a poor performer is worse than buying nothing at all. We make our money when we buy into a deal, so we will only purchase a property if we have room to juice our return. Often, we'll be interested in an asset, but the asking price will be too high. When we know we can't acquire it for a reasonable amount, we walk away, which we've done too many times to count. The temptation will be high, especially if you haven't purchased any real estate in a while, to overpay and brush the red flag under the rug. Don't let the real estate bug get the best of you. You must be disciplined in the practice of acquiring. Here are a few situations where passing on an opportunity was the best deal we could make.

A few years ago, we found ourselves fighting tooth and nail for a lucrative property that was being sold by a private group of investors looking to make headlines with a record-setting price. Our first all-cash offer got rejected. We liked the real estate, so we did something we don't often do: offered a higher bid. Again, rejected. At that point, it didn't pencil out to offer even one more dollar regardless of how badly we wanted the property. Due to the high likelihood of rising interest rates, we figured the price tag would probably decrease as potential buyers struggled to afford the expensive cost of a loan. I made a bet with myself that every six months the sellers would be in significantly worse shape and eventually list their property on the market again. If they do come running back to us, we'll offer them lower than our original bid.

Facing the harsh reality that a deal won't work and having the discipline to walk away will eventually manifest in a high-performing real estate portfolio. Shortly after we distanced ourselves from the bidding war, we started working with a broker based out of Dallas who showed us several new properties that we had to pass up on because the returns were too low. We stayed in touch with him and found out he actually used to live in Tulsa, which is how he knew about many of the transactions in our market. Eventually, he sent us the details of a profitable building on Seventy-First Street, in the heart of Tulsa, which fit our criteria to the T. We bought it within thirty days. Chances are high that if we caved on our original criteria or splurged on any of the prior options, we wouldn't have been able to purchase this stellar property. It will serve you well to create your own ten commandments of real estate, so you also won't be diverted by the next shiny object.

THE BREAKDOWN

t can be said that in every single product type, whether it's car washes, hotels, office, land, retail, self-storage, or any other type of real estate, an investor has made, or is making, a fortune worth many millions. There is no perfect complexion of properties to build a portfolio around. Each product has a unique and varying ability to cash flow, appreciate, and garner risk. It's up to you to learn as much about each as you can and make an educated decision for yourself. Just be sure to take into account your market's supply and demand at the time, your personal motivations, and your current skillset. Here is the breakdown of our company's real estate portfolio.

Retail strip centers. Most of what we own are smaller strip centers, which are non-grocery anchored properties. These assets differ from shopping centers, which house commercial grocery stores, like Costco or Kroger, in that they are usually smaller ticket deals, to the tune of $2 million to $4 million versus $10 million to $20 million. Although a shopping center can potentially be a safer asset because of a well-known anchor tenant's ability to drive business to a site, we choose to stay away from them. We don't want that much capital tied up in one location. For the price of one shopping center, we would rather diversify our risk over several decentralized strip centers. If a large shopping center runs into complications—for example, if ongoing construction slows business for a period of time, or if an anchor tenant vacates entirely—cash flow would dry up all at once. On the flip side, one temporarily underperforming strip center can be offset by the handful of others we own. The cash will keep flowing. That said, we try to play both sides by purchasing properties near, and in some cases directly in front of, larger shopping centers.

We've also never been interested in buying big-box malls. Amazon and online shopping have been strangling many of those owners. The tenants at our centers include larger retailers like Subway, GameStop, and Papa Johns, smaller mom-and-pop stores, as well as an increasing number of service-based tenants like hair salons, bike shops, and a vacuum repair store. These service-based tenants have proven resilient to the recent explosion of ecommerce. They're a hedge against product-based retailers going out of business in the future.

Pre-development land. In a market like Tulsa, with a surplus of green space, developing on raw land allows us to net the highest returns. We prefer to buy lots near stoplights on busy thoroughfares with high drive-by traffic. If the picture doesn't already look like that, we'll sit tight until population growth drives development outwards.

I'll tell you a good indicator of population growth: new housing subdivisions. We're currently holding onto a property near Bixby, Oklahoma, a city that's earned the nickname "Garden Spot of Oklahoma" for its lengthy history as a farming community. It remains one of the best places to grow and buy vegetables in the region. Bixby is also notorious for being one of the fastest growing cities in the state this past decade, and the second fastest growing in the Tulsa metro. City officials are driving transformation in the area, and residential developers are just starting to arrive on the scene. As they plan their upscale subdivisions, the city has called for A-class strip centers to meet the looming demand for conveniently-located shops.

We purchased our plot of land in Bixby from a wealthy individual who ran into health problems in his early nineties. He was willing to take a slight financial hit to cash out his fortune while he could still live to see it. Originally, he had paid around $950 thousand for the land. We bought it off him for $750 thousand. Our property is a stone's throw away from what will likely be engulfed by a sea of houses, on the corner of a four-way intersection. Once homeowners move in, they'll require nearby retail services. At that point, we'll start to build. All the property taxes we incur in the meantime will be covered by the first year's cash flow. We have good liquidity, so we aren't in any rush. If you don't have patience, don't buy virgin land.

A dentist owns and works out of the office that adjoins our lot in Bixby. He's playing with the thought of retiring as he grows older. Our team has made it a point to maintain an open line of communication with him. We've reminded him numerous times that we have an interest in buying him out. He's a rugged farm type of guy, skilled at his craft, but an unpredictable individual. Our team recently approached this dentist with a proposal letter and contract, expressing our willingness to pay the same price per square foot that we originally paid for our parcel. We considered this to be a fair offer given that our property is on the corner of the throughfare, accessible from every direction of the split four-lane road, which is much more valuable to a potential retail tenant than where his office is situated. Staying true to his unpredictable nature, he accepted the letter with a smile but refused to sign the contract. Adding the dentist's acreage to our parcel would make our future development significantly more valuable. For this reason, we'll revisit the conversation at a later time. Land is like a blank canvas; there is a lot you can do with it.

Our bread-and-butter lot size to build a strip center ranges from one to two acres. We only construct A-class buildings, as I've come to find that they have the highest quality with the fewest issues, using brick and stucco on the outside, which lasts long and looks good. Also, one trick I learned is to put in a concrete parking lot as opposed to an asphalt one. Concrete has superior longevity, and more importantly, an appraiser takes note of it in their evaluation. A higher evaluation allows us to justify charging tenants higher base rent. Land acquisitions and ground-up developments can be risky ventures, but they can offer some of the greatest payoffs in real estate. You are only limited by your creativity.

Net lease retail – triple net. A triple net (NNN) lease is a type of real estate lease where a tenant agrees to pay their pro-rata share of all operating expenses associated with property taxes, insurance, and common area maintenance (CAM), which includes maintenance, repair, and replacement. This is in addition to the predetermined base rent. Landlords in this structure bill their tenants back for all costs incurred in the categories mentioned above. Yearly increases are also typically added to the base rental rate to at least match inflation.

Many fast-food joints, formally known as quick service restaurants, such as Burger King, are on triple net leases, as well as many popular drug store chains like CVS, common convenience stores like Dollar General, and well-known auto shop chains like Jiffy Lube.

Our company owns a handful of quick service restaurants, including a Carl's Junior, which is on a triple net lease. Our tenant, Carl's Junior, agrees to pay us, the landlord, rent, including all the expenses pertaining to the property, in return for being able to conduct their fast-food operations out of our space. You might be wondering why Carl's Junior wouldn't just buy the real estate they use outright. It could be because they're targeting a specific customer or population demographic in an area that doesn't have any for-sale listings. It might be for the flexibility of being able to move locations if the desirability of their submarket changes. Or maybe it's all part of their strategic business plan to boost profits. From the standpoint of many retail tenants, they can achieve higher returns, starting in the double digits, by freeing up the dollars that they otherwise would've spent on a down payment or on annual interest payments from a mortgage loan. Renting allows them to deploy the extra cash right back into their profitable business as working capital. That's not to say all the retail giants rent. As of January 2022, McDonald's owns about 70 percent of the buildings they operate out of across their 39,000 locations worldwide. McDonald's has the cash to do so. However, it's important to remember that, even for a company as well established as they are, their primary business is still cooking retail food, not owning commercial real estate. That's our area of expertise. It's best to stick to what you know.

Net lease retail properties are generally sought after by investors for the completely passive ownership structure and long-term nature of the leases, with tenants locked in anywhere from ten to twenty years. The return is lower than most other real estate assets because of the minimal amount of management and risk required. That's not to say this product is risk free, especially for a single-tenant net lease property, meaning a standalone structure. The value of the asset is directly proportional to the amount of rental income it generates. If a landlord's only tenant vacates, without any more rent coming in the property will be worth pennies on the dollar to the market. This is why location is imperative to your success. If you acquire in a desirable location, tenants will be incentivized to re-lease your space. Worst-case scenario, if they ultimately pack up and leave, you will have a line of other suitors eager to sign a contract to gain access to the strategic merits of your site. Due to the lower associated return, the acquisition of net lease retail is a low priority for us right now. However, if we come across a good deal in a strong part of town, we won't hesitate to ride out the passive cash flow appreciation. This is the reason why we purchased a Burger King around the time of the 2008 housing crisis.

One unassuming morning years ago, a young New York broker from one of the large Fortune 500 firms cold-called me because he saw that I was a nearby owner to some new product he'd recently brought to market. He pitched me several "stellar" Burger Kings that were available to purchase, including one that neighbored a property our company already owned. The last one caught my attention. The parcel was just over an acre with a small single-tenant retail building situated on a thoroughfare. The property was adjacent to a corporately-owned Walmart that had previously bought all the surrounding land, set its store back from the main road, and sold the frontage to a pair of senior investors who owned and operated several Burger King franchises. Over the years the senior investors elected to buy some of the real estate they were operating out of. In light of the grim economy at the time, these mom-and-pop owners felt pressured to cash out some of their real estate holdings, pass on the day-to-day operations to their son, and formally retire. This New York sales broker was their way out.

There wasn't much more than country farmland surrounding the site, but I understood the potential of the area. I was confident that further development was imminent. Walmart wouldn't have invested millions into the location unless, based on their own research, they were similarly bullish. After taking a second look at the boundary lines of the property, I discovered an opportunity hidden in plain sight that sold me on the deal. Without a clear explanation, I pushed the broker to close as quickly as possible, in less than thirty days. I promised to reveal the reason for my haste once the asset was in our company's name.

After the property traded hands, the New York broker ringed me up. I later found out he had never been to Tulsa. I told him to pull up the aerial view of the property on Google Maps, which he hadn't thoroughly inspected. There was a sizeable portion of land next to the building that had never been developed, and it was included in the sale. The retail box covered about 60 percent of the lot, leaving 40 percent open for our team to add value. The Burger King tenant had a thirty-year lease with five-year options already locked in place, so they weren't going anywhere. However, our team could tear down the existing one-unit structure and include the Burger King on the end cap of a brand-new multi-tenant strip center. Our goal was to maximize the entire parcel and generate significantly more cash flow.

We bought this property for about $1 million around 2008. Due to the transformation of the overall economy, the yearly rental bumps, and the now heavily-trafficked, premier location, the real estate has appreciated significantly in value. Brokers call me every other week about selling it, with the last bid coming in almost three times what we paid for it. Once we complete the redevelopment, those offers will skyrocket.

Keeping our assets so close to home has allowed us to cover costs more effectively. It has also allowed us to fundamentally understand the terrain of our market, including both product and players, which has made it easier to uncover lucrative deals that others might've overlooked or missed altogether. Technically, you can own net lease retail all around the country due to the lack of time required to manage them. But, if you want to develop a long-term company, a dynasty, it'll serve you well to stay local so you can take advantage of the immense value hiding in plain sight.

TO MANAGE OR NOT
TO MANAGE

Establishing an internal property management component will benefit your real estate business in more ways than one. If you have the capability of handling many things in house, such as leasing, maintenance, and sub-contracting, then you will be able to cover costs more effectively, increase your returns, and better serve your tenants, who will choose to stay with you longer as a result.

The secret to our management team's success is that we only buy properties within close proximity to where we live. This strategy allows us to take advantage of economies of scale, which decreases our overall costs and boosts the company's profit margin. Our internal property managers live in Tulsa, and they handle our entire portfolio here. Whether our portfolio consists of two or twenty properties, their salaries are fixed. Each new acquisition we add to their oversight decreases the company's cost of management on a per property basis. Additionally, an effective property manager fixes problems and responds quickly, which is hard to do if they're based thousands of miles and countless hours away from their tenants. For these individuals, maintaining high standards will come at the additional cost of hiring external help, in the form of a third-party property manager.

The time and effort required to manage a property largely depends on the product type. In my experience, distant owners usually only have the capacity to manage passive real estate products like net lease retail. On the other end of the spectrum, multifamily managers get calls all hours of the day and night about something not working. They need to be within arm's reach. There is certainly money to be made with apartments, but getting a phone call on Saturday night doesn't sound appetizing to me. With our strip centers we usually only get calls during business hours throughout the week, which fits our style well.

If you aren't willing to manage your asset correctly, tenants will get frustrated and opt to vacate when their next option comes due. This will result in higher vacancy, lower returns, and a grungy reputation for your real estate business. In sum, if you do the job correctly and work with tenants to solve issues, an in-house property management capability will accelerate your cash flow. On the other hand, if you neglect repairs and communicate poorly in leasing, keeping things in house will only leave you with a swelling headache. In the latter scenario, it would be more advantageous to fork up the extra cash and hire a professional management company to keep your tenants happy and paying.

Picture for a moment that you have already connected with the movers and shakers in your market, saved cash, identified a great opportunity, and closed on a high-performing asset. At this point, if you are too busy with your primary career, or if you have little knowledge about managing real estate, you can hire a professional management group to serve your tenants and conduct leases, which, of course, they'll bill you for. This is a viable proposition for many. As you know, I did this for a year after buying my first retail center on South Peoria Avenue. It was a wise decision and worthwhile education. Eventually, as you become more experienced and as your company grows, you might consider hiring an employee or two to service all the assets under your name. This often comes at a dramatically reduced cost over the long term. Still, each additional employee you hire will increase complexity internally, as far as liability and communication are concerned, in the short term. For this reason, we have intentionally kept our management team small. We handle as much responsibility as we can internally and sub-contract out for additional jobs beyond our capability to third parties as needed. Keeping things in house has both juiced our returns and bolstered our daily operations.

"HOW MANY PROPERTIES DO YOU NEED TO ACHIEVE FINANCIAL FREEDOM?"

I f you're looking for a concrete number, it doesn't exist. Generating wealth from real estate has less to do with the sheer number of properties you own and much more to do with the quality of the deals you have. Specifically, I'm referring to how much rent you can demand, how effectively you can manage expenses, and what kind of margins, or return, you can realize over time. Of course, the latter will fluctuate depending on your debt obligations. I generally define a quality deal by three primary indicators: the capitalization rate at which you buy and sell the property, your return on investment (ROI), and your return on equity (ROE).

The value of a real estate property can be captured by the capitalization rate. This is a basic formula of the net operating income, which is the revenue the asset generates minus its expenses, accounting for vacancy, divided by the purchase price. This is likely the first metric you'll consider when evaluating a new acquisition, with a desirable capitalization rate being a higher percentage for the buyer, and the last metric you'll consider before cashing out of a deal, with a desirable capitalization rate being a lower percentage for the seller. This formula explicitly reflects the value, in terms of the earning capacity of a property, without taking into account how it was financed. By increasing rents, implementing strategic value add management, or by decreasing expenses, an investor can boost their net operating income and therefore the overall value of their property.

Imagine you're considering buying an existing building. You've already been told the asking price from the seller as well as the net operating income it produced for the year. With that common information in any sales transaction, you could easily solve for the capitalization rate at which you would be buying. This is depicted in the equation below. Because local real estate brokers track all recent trades, they have a good indication of what the typical range of capitalization rates are in your market. Their input can help you gauge whether you're looking at the deal of a lifetime or are about to get screwed over. The same formula, through simple math, can also be shifted around to show the value of a property that has no price tag on it. In other words, an off-market property. Say you were to drive by an unmarked building on which you wanted to make an offer. To ballpark what the property might be worth, you would make an assumption about the net income it generates and divide that figure by your local broker's best indication of the current capitalization rate.

$$\text{Capitalization Rate} = \text{Net Operating Income} / \text{Purchase Price}$$
$$\text{or}$$
$$\text{Purchase Price} = \text{Net Operating Income} / \text{Capitalization Rate}$$

Regarding ROI, our goal is to achieve at least a 10 percent return. Historically, over the last one hundred years, that's what has been gained on average out of an equity investment, as discussed in Chapter Seven. Most of the properties that our company has owned long term are exceeding that number because of equity growth, rent appreciation, and various improvements made to our properties that have since added value. For this reason, we realistically aim for a return on investment greater than 12 percent if it's a long-term hold. This equation has been listed below for reference.

$$\text{Return on Investment} = (\text{Current Value} - \text{Initial Equity}) / \text{Initial Equity}$$

The last quantitative metric, ROE, is another way of saying cash flow after debt service. This is the net operating income minus the annual debt payment, divided by the original equity placed in the deal. It's a reflection of the profitability of invested capital, which derives both the return on the asset itself and the way in which it was financed. This is commonly referred to as the cash-on-cash return.

We only leverage a small amount of debt when we buy, so this return metric often looks worse than our ROI because our equity, the denominator in the equation, is usually an increasingly large number over time. However, our company's primary emphasis is maximizing cash flow, and without an annual mortgage payment, our asset can do so at full capacity. For this reason, we aren't as concerned about what this metric looks like on paper.

$$\text{Return on Equity} = \text{Cash Flow After Debt Service} / \text{Equity}$$

To recap, quality deals are the key to wealth in real estate. Once you define what that means for you, which will likely involve setting targets for each metric above, try to accumulate only deals that fit the description. Depending on what you decide, financial freedom could be a matter of acquiring just two, or, in some cases, more than ten, real estate properties.

ELEVEN
OPM: OTHER PEOPLE'S MONEY

Side note from Terry:

The mindset for borrowing money to acquire real estate is intuitive: contractually agree to buy an asset for X amount and leverage Y dollars from someone else to pay X. The benefit of using other people's money comes at the cost of the interest rate, also known as the cost of capital. This concept isn't rocket science, but in practice, it can be tricky to understand which kind of financing tools to use and how much capital to borrow. Best practice will largely be indicative of your personal risk preference and real estate strategy. The following is a dictation of my own approach to financing investment real estate.

THE TOOLS

High level, my strategy involves borrowing a relatively short-term loan that I will be able to pay off fast, even if it costs me a little more up front to hedge the extra risk. My goal is to release all lender claims on my property as quickly as possible to achieve outright ownership and maximum cash flow output. The granular details of your loan will make or break the feasibility of any project. Understanding these details and putting the right mechanics in place is imperative. Here is a brief explanation of the most important things I consider.

The faster you can throw a lender off your back, the better. If I can't negotiate the flexibility of paying a debt off early, preferably any time without incurring a prepayment penalty, I will, at the very least, try to implement a fully amortizing repayment structure that will allow me to own an asset free and clear by the last day of the loan term. Amortization is the process of paying off a debt with regular payments. If the regular payments reduce the loan balance, including all principal and interest, to zero by the end of the term, then it has a fully amortizing payment structure. This is the safer, and my first, choice. The alternative structures are partially amortizing, negatively amortizing, or interest only. Basically, all these alternatives mean is that the principal loan balance will *not* be completely paid off by the end of the loan term. Either a lump sum balloon payment will be required to repay the debt back in full on the last day, or a new loan will have to be taken out to replace the old one, also known as a refinance. Investors sometimes prefer these alternative structures since they result in smaller monthly payments. Although they may be ideal for a bridge to stabilization project, an ongoing construction, or for a property that isn't generating any income, they are riskier options that work against outright ownership.

Most loans that aren't fully amortizing also carry variable interest rates. This means that the rate you agree to pay at closing is tied to an agreed upon financial index like the London Interbank Offered Rate (LIBOR), which is subject to change. Of course, there is a chance your rate could go down over the term, in which case you would realize a net benefit, but that is a risky bet. Variable rate loans have jeopardized a tremendous amount of real estate investors due to the 2022–2023 rate hikes initiated by the Fed to combat inflation. With a variable rate, one month you could be fine, and the next you could be in well over your head. Have no doubt about it, lenders can be great white sharks. Once they smell blood and start circling, it never ends well. By and large, locking in a fixed rate is the safest way to play the game. This means that the rate you agree upon at closing will be the same figure used to calculate interest for the entire loan term. It will not fluctuate even if the market does.

The perfect loan doesn't always exist. You might want five enhancements. Depending on your property, the current market, and the purpose of your loan, a lender might only be willing to give you two or three. It's often a push-pull dynamic. For example, a lender may offer you a low fixed interest rate, but at the cost of locking you into a longer term, with penalties for paying off the debt early. Conversely, in return for offering you a short-term loan without any prepayment penalties, a lender may require you to accept a partial or interest only amortization structure with a variable interest rate. It's not an exact science. As long as you have a clear end goal driving your strategy, which for me is outright ownership and maximum cash flow output, you can negotiate something to reasonably accommodate your most important needs.

Around 2012, the financing tool our company used to acquire our Brooktown strip center was a loan from an insurance company. We were able to negotiate a great fixed rate for this one; however, we had to accept a ten-year term with massive prepayment penalties. To clarify, the rate was favorable at the time we locked it in almost a decade ago. From that point until 2021, rates started depressing, so it seemed like we were losing. In 2022, rates began to skyrocket, so we were back to being grateful for what we had. The beauty of a fixed rate is not having to worry about stressful fluctuations. We were also able to lock in a fully amortizing structure on this one. Although it has resulted in larger annual payments than the alternative interest-only or partial amortization structures, which temporarily strained our cash flow, as of a few months ago the loan was repaid in full. We now own the strip center free and clear. The strip center has become another part of our money-making machine, able to print cash at its full capacity. A financing tool is only as good as the sum of its parts. Now that you know some of the inputs that make a good tool, here are a few finished products we use and where to get them.

We typically turn to commercial banks for smaller short-term loans. These are the majority we've held in the past. One of our company's only current forms of borrowing as of this writing is a line of credit I personally guarantee from my local bank. This financing tool allows our team to immediately take out significant dollars like a credit card as long as the line is kept open. The bank reviews my income and net worth statement on an annual basis to confirm that I have enough assets backing me to keep it that way. Credit lines usually have variable rates and no prepayment penalties, so we prioritize paying these off first when we draw on them.

Our team also routinely pulls money out of one of our smaller strip centers in Claremore, a compact suburb of Tulsa, via a standard bank refinance. This is a high performing piece of collateral in a strong market that we have a lot of built-up equity in. We've borrowed against it several times. The bank has a firm understanding of its value.

A strong relationship with a bank is priceless. I've worked with some of the principals on the loan committee board of Bank of Oklahoma for over fifteen years with a clean record. A bank that can see you successfully execute your strategy numerous times will not hesitate to loan you money with accretive terms. They'll get comfortable with how you operate and will be willing to work with you to fix problems that arise. This will allow you to shrink a bank's credit approval timelines, strike quickly on lucrative opportunities, and make challenging deals work.

If a commercial bank is the solution we turn to in the short term, an insurance company is our solution in the long term. Our past insurance company loan, that we recently paid off, had a term of ten years and couldn't be prepaid without incurring a hefty penalty. It carried a fixed rate, which is always a safer bet in a rising interest rate environment, but the trade-off was that this lender locked us in for a longer time period. For this reason, an insurance company isn't our first choice. Depending on the deal, an insurance company can also offer variable rate short-term loans of five years or less, although we haven't personally used those.

This section barely scratches the surface of the multitude of lenders and financing tools available. Some are better than others. We've found the most success with the above, but that varies by strategy. It would be wise to educate yourself on all the options you have and how to use them to reach your real estate goals as you become a more serious player in the space.

The beauty of financing is that, unlike a cut-and-dry math problem, there can be multiple right answers. You don't just have to use a line of credit from a bank, an insurance loan, or any other type of leverage alone. You can mix and match different tools to fit the deal at hand. It doesn't need to be pretty. It just needs to get the job done. If you have the right tools, you can fix any job. Hopefully this added a few to your growing tool belt.

LAW OF LEVERAGE

U nless you're Jeff Bezos, you will need to borrow something to buy real estate. Even if you were as wealthy as he, you would probably still want to borrow some amount to make your capital work hardest for you. That said, leverage can work both ways. If used wisely it can be like the turbo charger to your V10 investment engine. If misused, it can be like excessively revving the engine before popping it into gear, blowing out the transmission of your wealth-building real estate vehicle.

Generally, when a lender originates a loan, the associated interest rate they charge reflects their outlook on the market, the acute risks associated with you as a guarantor, and the feasibility of your specific deal. A basic rule of thumb is that the higher degree of leverage you assume, in other words, purchasing a property with a higher loan-to-value ratio, the higher your interest rate and annual payment will be. The benefit of borrowing 80 percent of the appraised value of a property, an 80 percent loan-to-value, will come at a higher cost than borrowing 50 percent of the appraised value of a property, a 50 percent loan-to-value. Although the latter option will require you to put down more cash equity at the start, the reoccurring debt payments will be less expensive.

The Law of Leverage is the hallmark of my real estate strategy on which everything else is built. It's my answer to the question of precisely how much to borrow. The Law of Leverage is the principle of growing a portfolio from a position of high equity and through cash flow generation rather than by heavily borrowing. In practice, instead of acquiring three investment properties quickly without fully paying off any of them and by borrowing 80-90 percent of the aggregate appraised value, I'd buy one or two investment properties with a small loan, say 30 percent aggregate loan-to-value, and only move on to the third and fourth properties after paying off the first two completely. I assume a small loan amount relative to the equity I put in and aggressively pay down what little debt I have with the income my properties generate. This practice has allowed me to dramatically increase my ownership stake in each deal, decrease the risk of not being able to cover my debt obligations, and maximize the cash flowing potential of my entire real estate portfolio.

You may be thinking, "Gee, this sounds like a reasonable strategy, but wouldn't utilizing higher leverage to acquire several properties at once be a more efficient path to wealth accumulation?" In the beginning, it might seem to be the case. Technically, you would own a larger pool of properties in a shorter period of time, but don't be deceived. In that situation, the lender would own you. Your ownership stake will always be lower by adding debt to debt. Due to the expensive interest cost you'll be required to pay each year by aggressively levering up, your cash flow will also suffer dramatically. That's a zero-sum game that will cause your net worth to stagnate and slowly decrease over time.

When you're young and strapped for cash, you may need a bigger loan to purchase your first few properties. That's okay. As your portfolio grows, if it were me, I would do so by putting down greater equity from the start or by purchasing my properties outright before mounting debt on debt, even though it will require more time to build momentum. Here's the kicker. As driving downhill requires incrementally less energy, this wealth building strategy picks up steam fast and requires less effort with each new cash flowing property you add to your portfolio. If the results of abiding by the Law of Leverage were graphed, with years on the x-axis and dollars on the y, you would see the trendline take on an increasingly steeper convex shape over time. Most importantly, the Law of Leverage will protect you from one of the deadliest risks to real estate investors, as seen through the housing crisis of 2008 and most recently the COVID-19 pandemic: being unable to repay a debt obligation due to a rising interest rate environment or a lull in revenue as the result of an unpredictable market downturn. What follows is foreclosure and bankruptcy. Game over.

Mark Twain, the prolific American writer and poet, famously wrote, "Whenever you find yourself on the side of the majority, it is time to pause and reflect." When the economy is flourishing, and everyone around you is leveraging up, stop. While most people are only focused on soaking up the sun while it's shining, very few use that beautiful weather to prepare for the storm that is inevitably going to come. Remember, markets are cyclical by nature. The years of 2006 and 2007 were characteristic of warm sunny days that most investors spent soaking up ridiculous loans, between 90-100 percent loan-to-value. These individuals probably thought, "What could go wrong?" 2008 hit their financial stature like a freight train, causing so many people to default that it sent the entire nation into a recession.

More recently, during the bull market of early September 2019, when the stock market was reaching new highs on a weekly basis, and interest rates were hovering at record lows, I witnessed tons of frivolous private and institutional investors mounting their real estate debt loads. Many opted for low down payments and variable interest rates. Making money was easy, or so they thought. They must've forgotten that just one meeting of the Federal Reserve could put them completely out of business. Sure enough, in 2022, following a slew of interest rate hikes aimed at subduing rampant inflation, owners of all product types with variable rate loans started to feel the burn. Many are now unable to cover their debts heading into the new year. They will either have to come out of pocket, sell their property at a loss, or declare bankruptcy and hand the keys over to their lender. The Law of Leverage means borrowing no more than you would reasonably be able to pay back given a rising interest rate environment.

When the market booms, it is theoretically a safer time to borrow, but you should never violate your Law of Leverage. Stay levelheaded through the hype. Take the necessary precautions to cushion your portfolio from rising interest rates. Saving money diligently is one way to do this. Establishing a conservative debt-to-equity ratio from the start is the most effective way. Most people consider 50 percent to be reasonable. On the leverage spectrum, we prefer to sit in the low to moderate end. In relation to the value of our entire portfolio, that means between 20-30 percent. Our Law of Leverage states that we should never exceed that. In 2019, our total leverage was between 2-5 percent, so virtually none. According to our law, we actually had the room to be more effective in how we acquired our next few assets with a higher debt-to-equity ratio, using more of other people's money. This would be a safe bet because we would essentially be adding debt to a position of high equity. If we were sitting on a cumulative debt load equal to 30 percent of the value of our portfolio, and then we acquired an additional property with, say, a 60 percent loan-to-value, which exceeds our guideline, we would instead be adding debt to debt. That is the trap to avoid. With one market swing we could be in over our heads with the potential of losing everything. That takes the control out of our hands and places it in the unpredictable grip of the market. Constantly reinforce the walls of your real estate portfolio. If you don't, you will be throwing stones in a glass house. We all know how that drama ends.

The Law of Leverage also means borrowing no more than you would reasonably be able to pay back given a sudden decline in cash flow due to a lull in occupancy and revenue. In 2020, the COVID pandemic revealed the true value of this unwritten law. In the course of a couple weeks, all in-person business, travel, recreation, and production came to a screeching halt, the S&P 500 index lost all of its tremendous gains from the prior five years combined, and the economy shut down indefinitely. The long-term repercussions following such a dramatic economic shift are still unfathomable. In the short term, some unfortunate multifamily owners saw their tenants protected by government moratoriums that allowed them to forgo paying rent without being evicted while office landlords saw their tenants fold on their leases and vacate entirely. Depending on the product type, base rent collection, one of the main drivers of cash flow, came to a dizzying halt. I imagine some new gray hairs emerged on the scalps of those owners. What highly-leveraged real estate investors learned the hard way, and what you should ask yourself, is this, "Does a rogue tenant that breaks their lease get a landlord off the hook for repaying their obligation to a lender?" When a tenant vacates a property, they can go out and find another home. When a loan is defaulted on, a landlord loses their home. The lender will fight tooth and nail to claw back their capital. If an owner can't come out of pocket, best believe their property, or worse, will be on the chopping block.

Let's paint a very real picture to zero in on the point to be made. Meet Bill, the investor who borrowed excessively while the market was booming pre-pandemic, who didn't save much in the way of liquid reserves and was solely dependent on the rent collection from his retail tenants to cover the large monthly mortgage payments he owed his lender. Because he over-leveraged while rates were low, when COVID shut the nation down and his revenue dried up for months on end, he was forced to pick between two rotten options. He could either continue paying the principal and interest out of pocket, to the tune of tens or even hundreds of thousands of dollars, to keep control of the property, or he could cut his losses and default on the loan. The latter would mean giving up control of his investment property altogether. It was a lose-lose situation for that sorry soul.

Now let's analyze the options an investor who abided by their Law of Leverage, who only borrowed a miniscule loan relative to their overall equity in the property, or paid all cash from the start, faced in a similar situation. Nick was an owner who avoided holding onto any kind of serious debt obligation, even during the historically low-rate environment of 2019, who diligently saved liquid reserves for a rainy day. He prepared his real estate portfolio for the worst. Once COVID hit his retail tenants equally as hard as it hit Bill's, and they ceased paying rent, he never found himself in a situation where he'd have to default. He didn't make any bonus during that period either, which is by no means an ideal situation. However, he avoided the stressful fear of losing his real estate asset to a hungry lender. Falling back on the cashflow generated by his other fully paid off properties, Nick found himself in the unique position of being relatively cash heavy during a time when most other investors, like Bill, were cash light. After a few months passed, Nick came across his counterpart's property at auction, which was defaulted on shortly after the closures began. He decided to buy it since it was being offered at a fraction of what it would have cost on the competitive market a year prior. Nick, the Law of Leverage abiding investor, ended up adding another lucrative asset to his portfolio, instead of recording a staggering blow like Bill. A drama like this has occurred in every down market in history. Some of the most successful real estate professionals will reveal that their best deals came in an economy that was similarly flat on its back. Don't be a Bill.

Leverage too much and you risk default. Leverage too little and you're sacrificing an incredibly powerful tool unique to real estate that can make your money work twice as hard as you do. The truth lies in the middle of the two extremes. By and large, less debt leaves you better off, but some conservative debt can be accretive to your position. Become fluent in leverage and the cost of capital to maximize the benefit of borrowing money to acquire or develop real estate. Most importantly, establish your own Law of Leverage. You will live and die by it.

BREAKING THE LAW OF LEVERAGE: A COVID SHORT STORY

March 2020:

"**H**ighly-leveraged owners are getting squeezed by their 80-90 percent loan-to-value debt obligations. Their demand for cash is great. They have left themselves with little wiggle room to maneuver through this crisis. We will likely see foreclosures soon. The two questions every owner is asking themselves right now are, "How much rent do I have to lose before it impinges my debt payments?" and "How long will this pandemic last?" Our team has a significant safety margin so these are questions we will not be losing sleep over.

Our company's low leverage will give us breathing room if our own revenue decreases. We may not set any records this year, but we sure as hell won't lose any of our assets or have legal action taken against us by a bank for not paying. We will live to fight another day."

June 2020:

"We just received our first rent setbacks after agreeing to give a few of our strip center tenants reductions. Our triple net properties are also getting hit hard as fewer people leave their homes. Carl's Junior notified us that it needs to suspend payment. We're going to counter with the option to defer rent, meaning they'll still have to pay, but they'll have more time to do so. These complications come with the business. Disastrous problems arise when landlords with staggering debt loads face a lull in cashflow. Once they start hurting, they lack the flexibility to work toward a win-win solution with their tenants, an outcome that would otherwise only benefit both parties for the long term, especially once the pandemic becomes a blip in the rearview mirror. Maintaining a healthy amount of leverage, erring on the conservative side when in doubt, has allowed our team to be more effective problem solvers as we've faced these acute tenant issues. It has also put us in a position to buy other people's problems.

There have been times where we've acquired four properties in a year, and some years where we didn't even buy one. We have a high cash flow business because we don't overpay for our properties. We also don't have massive loan payments to make because we put up such high equity from the start. Our business model revolves around maximizing cash flow generation. We have enough on hand to pull the trigger if an A-class strip center comes available at a discount. I have no doubt a select group of real estate investors will capture a great score as we emerge from the tight grip of COVID-19. Our company's goal will be to solidify a top spot on that elite roster."

August 2020:

"Things will pick up, but right now business is slow. In Sand Springs, for a strip center we recently constructed, we've decided to wait a year before signing any new leases, or at least until the market stabilizes. Every three to six months we will reassess the damage and go from there. We're also putting the brakes on another project we were otherwise ready to break ground on. This isn't a major concern because we bought the land all cash. We don't have any lenders breathing down our necks.

I expect the real estate industry to be rocky for the coming months as the market adjusts to the dramatic shocks it has absorbed. For investors with low debt loads, it should be nothing more than a temporary inconvenience. These individuals will be able to ride out the high vacancies without the pressure of looming debt payments. This is the biggest advantage of not borrowing excessively."

June 2021:

"Remember the development project we put on pause less than a year ago? Well now it's full speed ahead. We were able to lease 60 percent of the space, so we decided to finish the build. The market has been scary at times, but we've been well covered each step of the way. With leverage, when in doubt, always hang your hat on the conservative number.

To be clear, the Law of Leverage isn't an original idea from me. I learned it from others who, at the time, were far more wealthy and real estate savvy than I was. After experiencing the value of abiding by it for myself, I made it a point to never forget this incredible principle. For the sake of your own real estate dynasty, I hope you don't either."

PART FIVE

LIFE

TWELVE
EIGHTY-FIVE YEARS

"The people who are crazy enough to think they can change the world are the ones who do."
– Steve Jobs

"Never give up on something you can't go a day without thinking about."
– Winston Churchill

"It's the possibility of having a dream come true that makes life interesting."
– Paulo Coelho

CONDUCTING YOUR SYMPHONY

Countless noises ring in your ears daily; each beckoning for a piece of your finite time and energy. As the conductor of your own world-class life symphony, you can turn the endless array of noises into either a synergistic masterpiece or a mind-numbing dissonance. Deciding where to place your focus is an essential step to accomplishing anything worthwhile. Set your priorities straight so you can spend your time on what matters most.

Your priorities will evolve as you transition through the various stages of your life. When you're single, you can put in any kind of hours at work without igniting much conflict amongst those around you. Being single grants you the unique flexibility and freedom to do as you please. As you mature, you may desire the deep satisfaction that comes with marrying a long-term partner and working together to raise a family. These stages complement each other. There's room for both. That said, when you enter the latter stage of life, you'll have to be more strategic in how you split your time. No partner will be thrilled with a workaholic that subordinates time spent with them or the family. If you don't constantly adapt your schedule so that your time and attention adequately mirror your changing hierarchy of priorities, your symphony will have a dizzying effect on yourself and everyone around you.

It took me decades to master my life's orchestra. Early in my career I was always out of the house. I put in long hours, starting at 8:00 am, and because of evening meetings, I usually wouldn't return home until 10:00 pm. As I got older, I had to adjust my work-life balance, most dramatically when I settled down with my wife, and later when I had children. Doing so has preserved my most cherished relationships.

I currently prioritize the bulk of my life between the buckets of career and family with consistent time set aside for recharging my overworked mind. Interacting with my amazing laboratory staff is an invigorating experience while I'm on the hospital campus, but I try not to bring work home with me anymore. Once I get home, I silence that noise, shifting my focus to orchestrating a loving relationship with my family and growing my vitality through leisure. During the week, I'll sit down and have a Manhattan in the evening, reflect on the events of the day with my wife, listen to the news, and relish a home-cooked meal. I also record a few of my favorite shows so I can treat myself to some form of entertainment before bed. Constant mental and physical activity can get stressful. I've learned to manage it by gifting myself time in the evening to release pressure. I've come to understand that my workload will still be there when I awake each morning. It won't be going anywhere, even though sometimes I wish it would.

If you've gone numb to the song that is currently ringing out of your life's symphony, take a moment to stop and listen. You may find that the loudest noises commanding the bulk of your time are senseless distractions. Because you are the conductor, you have the power to adjust the tune, and your focus, at any moment.

LONGEVITY

I attribute my good health to constant physical and mental activity. When I was younger, farming, machinery work, and training young horses kept me in shape. In my mid-eighties, I do less taxing work, but I still work out with weights and on the cardio machine in my exercise room every weekend. During the week, while I'm at the lab, I escape from my office at some point in the day to walk the twelve-acre campus. Always stay active. Once you find yourself sitting around, that's when your body starts to deteriorate. It's a grim process.

Longevity also requires constantly exercising your mind. You must engage in mental workouts too. This is the reason I continue to work. Daily challenges at the lab stimulate my mind. They keep me growing as opposed to withering away. Anything you don't use, you will lose. This goes for both the mind and the body. It's the basis for the longevity I've experienced.

"WHAT DO YOU VALUE MOST IN LIFE?"

Family comes first. I'm ecstatic about having all my kids and grandkids within the borders of the same city limits. In the beginning, there was no chance they would've stayed so close to home. Some moved away. I never allowed myself to make that decision for them. They needed to discover their own path. Forcing someone to do what they don't want to has a polarizing effect. I did drop subtle hints until my family chose to come back home. All I had to do was give them an incentive.

I'm proud that despite our stresses and strains, we still enjoy each other's company. Unfortunately, it's somewhat commonplace today for a child or a few members to divert from the collective. They'll put pressure on their familial ties. Hopefully the others will still stick together. The bond of blood is one of the rarest types to come by. It's a finite resource. In my personal life, this support system has carried me through the deepest and darkest chasms that seemed unfathomable to traverse alone. My life hasn't been a bowl of cherries, but I can tell you, I've had the best of times and the worst of times with my family. Although you're not always going to be successful at keeping your family together, there are big advantages to giving it your best shot.

One of the greatest tests of a family's strength comes after the parents pass on. My older sister, Jean, and I share an intimate relationship that has remained untarnished since we were little kids. We have a profound loyalty to one another and a mutual trust that grows stronger every year. Family was one of the core values of our parents' overarching philosophy. I believe this bond was initiated by them. At a young age, they revealed to my sister and me the incredible power of tightly interwoven family ties. Through the experience of my lowest moments, I began to scratch the surface of the magic they were referring to. This understanding blossomed as I transitioned into parenthood, where I realized how important it is to always give your best, especially with kids. My emphasis has now shifted to spreading the secret power I discovered as a boy to my own family, with the hope that it will flourish throughout our future generations, as well as yours. Family is pure gold, more valuable than money or fame. If there is a disconnect in your life, it's worth it to do what you can to aid in the healing process. Family is as vital to me as personal health and time itself.

FIFTY-SEVEN YEARS

To give you some perspective on how I think about romantic relationships, this is how I met my wife. In the early 1960s, my brother-in-law, Tim, was an anesthesiologist who worked with a neurosurgeon, Dr. Wu, out of the same Kansas City hospital. Today, doctors take fully electronic x-ray images, but back then, they used physical film from a Kodak camera. As a result, there was a brief delay in each case when the pictures had to be developed in a darkroom over in radiology. While Dr. Wu stepped out to analyze the film, Tim, the lead anesthesiologist, and Mary Beth, the neurosurgical scrub nurse, would stay in the operating room to monitor the patient who was still asleep under anesthesia. Tim got to know Mary Beth since Dr. Wu repeatedly asked him to assist his cases. One day, Tim struck up a light-hearted conversation about Christmas plans during one of these breaks. Mary Beth mentioned she was in between boyfriends and was planning on spending the holiday alone. That night, over typical dinner conversation with his wife, my older sister Jean, this bright nurse got brought up. To Tim's surprise, Jean mentioned they went to the same nursing school and that she had actually met Mary Beth at an alumni event. My sister and brother-in-law started to scheme. The next day, Tim approached Mary Beth and explained the connection. Then he offered, "I have a brother-in-law coming to town to visit family for the holidays. He doesn't have much to do while he's here either. Would you be open to meeting him?" With a slight, somewhat awkward, hesitation she responded, "I'll consider it." Tim returned home that night with her phone number.

I was a young physician in my mid-twenties, single, and had everything going for me. I had a girlfriend in Omaha, where I went to medical school, and one in New York City. My options were open in Kansas City. I was playing the field and succeeding. I didn't need, or want, anyone else's help in finding a long-term partner. At the time, I wasn't sure I was ready for the lifelong commitment. My mother and sister were always playing matchmaker, determined to find me someone to settle down with. When Tim handed me Mary Beth's phone number, that was the first woman my brother-in-law ever suggested I take a chance on. I believed he had impeccable judgment because he picked my sister, whom I thought the world of, as a partner, so I agreed to give this mystery woman a call upon my return.

I visited Kansas City for the Christmas season during my first year in the U.S. Public Health Service residency program. Without much in the way of expectations, Mary Beth and I casually met up for a few hours at a local bar. Every night for the rest of the trip we went out together, except for one day near the end when I had to visit the girl I was still seeing in Omaha. There was nothing scandalous about it. Mary Beth knew where I was going, and meanwhile she had a date with an old college friend of mine. We were transparent with each other, which kept us on the same page. I took Mary Beth out one last time that holiday break before flying back to the East Coast. I had already made a commitment to a New Year's Eve date in New York City. It was a hectic time, to say the least. I continued to call Mary Beth throughout my second year in Staten Island. Once I left for sea, she did something that no other woman had ever done for me.

Although I emerged physically unscathed from the shipwreck in the North Atlantic, my mind carried hidden scars. Coming that close to dying brings everything home. I felt more mature and ready to commit to a greater purpose. This was a turning point in my life. I came back to port to a pile of letters Mary Beth had written to me each day I was gone. After I got back to my apartment and read every single one, I began to realize just how special this woman was. My Omaha girlfriend was, quite frankly, a little nuts, and the one in New York had family drama, but Mary Beth didn't have any of that baggage, plus she wrote to me every day. She had a unique way of expressing her love.

Our entire crew was given time off to recover from our seabound adventure, so I flew back to Kansas City that March. I don't know what got into either of us. We hardly knew each other, but at that point I asked her to marry me. To my surprise, she said yes. That June she flew out to New York City for a couple weeks to visit, and we were married that August. Neither of us recommend tying the knot that quickly. In retrospect, and both of us feel the same way, we had experienced enough men and women to understand what we were looking for. Back then it was common for people to get married between eighteen and twenty years old. Mary Beth was twenty-five, I was turning twenty-eight, and it felt right for both of us. My near-death experience on the East Coast brought me down to earth. It helped me realize that a life spent with someone you love is more fulfilling than several surface-level relationships or becoming self-absorbed with your career in quiet isolation.

I don't think I, or anyone else for that matter, can point to a perfect age to get married with the highest probability of success. I'd wager that cementing a permanent relationship starting at or after your mid- to late-twenties will offer you the best odds. Having some extra time to mature before tying the knot will allow you to gain the necessary experience to overcome the complicated challenges that come with romantic relationships. The more experience you have, the better off you'll be, as long as you are able to start each relationship with a clean slate, leaving old expectations and heavy baggage from the past behind. The lessons learned will shape you into a better life partner and refine the criteria you look for in others.

In romantic relationships we tend to ignore our partner's weaknesses and overemphasize their strengths. No one is perfect. It's essential to address the red flags early on to prevent resentment from building. You can't change anyone by sheer will, so, before going all the way, decide if you can live with someone as they are, despite their drawbacks. Although coming to this conclusion takes time, there is a point beyond which to settle down. Sometimes life will naturally open your eyes to when the time is right, like how the dramatic events at sea influenced me. Other times you will have to take a shot in the dark. Once you commit to taking the plunge, give it all you got. When conflicts arise, work with your partner to find solutions rather than splitting immediately.

I see a lot of couples today that don't stick it out long enough. Ups and downs are baked into every type of relationship. When the boat starts rocking, you've got to hold on tight and try to patch the holes rather than abandoning ship at the first opportunity. It's both necessary and beneficial for couples to work out disagreements together, in a mature manner. Those that consistently hear each other out and seek to better understand the other side will develop a deep mutual respect that will transform relationship-killing arguments into the glue that will keep the union intact. Ironically, disagreements are a blessing. A relationship without them would be unhealthy at worst and boring at best. Disagreements allow us to express our unique perspectives. They help us learn from and about one another. However, most people struggle to communicate respectfully. They often let their emotions take the driver's seat in tense conflicts.

The centerpiece to my philosophy on long-term romantic relationships is this: a healthy romantic relationship helps both parties grow. The union should make the two greater as a whole rather than as separate entities. This is why divorce never came into the conversation for my wife and me. Of course, we've had arguments, but we both believed that by sticking it out for the long term, we would be stronger, happier, and more powerful as a team than as isolated individuals. It has, therefore, been advantageous for us to weather every storm. I believe once married partners no longer feel the power of oneness, that is the point of no return. Divorce will likely manifest sooner or later.

I also believe there are situations where two people must come to accept that they aren't as compatible as they initially thought. Once the continuation of the union hinders the well-being and growth of both partners, it becomes detrimental to their individual development. It may be in the best interest of all parties to end the relationship; however, this realization can only come after both sides try their hardest to make things work. Divorce is a death sentence for the marriage, with complex repercussions. You have to be sure you are making the right call, especially when kids are involved. It requires investing time and sincere effort to get through challenges as a team first.

There is no magic to a long-term relationship. It isn't all sunshine and rainbows. The best way I can put it is that it's worth it. The right one works wonders, finding the right one is a time-consuming task, and you will never know your partner as well as you might think. Before committing your life to anyone, make sure they check the boxes of the nonnegotiable qualities you value most and accept that eventually, the person you thought you knew will become a stranger. Be prepared to stick out the disagreements as you reacquaint yourself with the new, and greater, person they are becoming. I've never regretted the decision I made fifty-seven years ago.

REGRET

The severity of mistakes and the regret you'll later suffer is directly proportionate to the importance of the situation. Regret is a matter of perspective. It blossoms out of overlooked mistakes. As I said, I've made more mistakes than I can remember. Fortunately, in the most important areas of my life, relating to my wife and kids, I made sure I got it right. For the other times where I missed the mark, I quickly learned.

In business, you will always have regrets. I don't care who you are, you're going make mistakes. Once you become a leader, each one will become an elephant in the room. I constantly reiterate to my team that, with as many decisions as I make in a day, it's impossible to be right on every one. The key is to identify which ones are wrong, to fix them at light speed, and to derive valuable lessons that will prevent you from becoming a repeat offender. That's how you can transmute a failure into a success.

I've made it a habit not to let regret fester inside me like the disease it is. Instead of avoiding ownership of painful or embarrassing mistakes, I address them. I starve the beast that is regret of time, which it so desperately needs to build shelter in my mind, until it dissipates altogether. To do this effectively you have to be open to your own imperfections and willing to right your wrongs. I dwell, especially in the evening, on the wrong decisions I made each day. Most are insignificant, but I never write any off. Fixing them will be priority number one when my eyelids crack open the morning following that realization. No matter what industry you operate in, understand that at some point you will have to be a firefighter, at least figuratively. It will serve you well to extinguish the flames of mistakes before they burn down the building, in other words, your sanity. Step one is yanking the fire alarm.

You've got nothing to lose by admitting your wrongdoings, except maybe damaged pride, and everything to gain by making them right. There is a saying that the fear of making a mistake is sometimes worse than the mistake itself. I would go as far as to say the fear of admitting you made a mistake is sometimes worse than the mistake itself. However, by acknowledging a mistake, you regain the power to make it right.

When you make a mistake, you are always better off fixing it quickly and admitting your faults rather than letting it go unaddressed. Every secret is eventually brought to light. When the people around you figure out you screwed up and that you didn't have the courage or character to do anything about it, the damage to your reputation will be irreversible. Publicly acknowledge mistakes as they come, fix them, learn from them, and your life regrets will be few and far between. That's the real prescription for a restful night's sleep.

NO LIFE WITHOUT DEATH

As a pathologist, I diagnose people with potentially fatal diseases. I see the grim reaper daily, and believe me, he's not a pretty sight. The thing an outsider must ask themselves is, how do I, or any other pathologist, mentally handle it? The saving grace is that we work behind the scenes, rarely getting to know our patients personally. Our lab performs over ten million tests a year, and we only communicate with a patient's middleman, their doctor, when results are ready to be sent back. Throughout the process, we try not to remember names. In staff discussions we'll only refer to patients by their disease.

Because I started my career in internal medicine where patient care was ingrained in my DNA, I still occasionally visit private hospital rooms. During these face-to-face meetings, I'll usually be joined by the patient's family, sometimes up to eight members, with agony in their eyes. They'll drill me with tough questions in rapid succession, for thirty minutes at a time, trying to understand their loved one's odds of survival. As emotionally heavy as these experiences are, I see them as opportunities to gift the family, as well as the patient, clarity during utterly uncertain situations. For this reason, I will continue to make these visits.

Over the years, I've learned that as soon as a patient hears the news of their fatal diagnosis, they don't process anything else. When I see them next, I must walk through the arduous conversation a second time. Upon receiving a death sentence, after the intense shock initially radiates through their body, a patient's goals undergo a rapid transformation as they reorient themselves to the time they may or may not have left to set things right in their life. Maybe there was something the patient always had a burning desire to do, something they never got to say to someone, relationships they needed to heal, challenges they wanted to overcome, or a passion they wanted to pursue before their time was up. Although these priorities finally made it to the top of list, they may have been put off until tomorrow one day, or one decade, too long. With the end in clear sight, these patients are often utterly helpless, both physically and mentally, to accomplish their goals. The good news for you is that you don't have to wait for a dreadful death sentence to come to this realization. I'd suggest taking a more progressive approach to life and acknowledge your own mortality right now. I would then use this voluntary epiphany to reevaluate your goals. This is not something to put on the backburner.

I've witnessed many patients die from fatal illness, and, at my age, most of my long-time friends have passed on. I look around these days and see so many starry-eyed young people. I've come to see death in a new light. I now understand that it's an integral part of the life cycle, crucial to the evolution of our species. The reality of life is death. They are one and the same, inseparable.

A veteran doctor once joked to me that there are only three things you're guaranteed in this life: death, taxes, and committee work. The first word stuck with me. Genetics can affect the timeline, but an end to life is a universal reality. You have no reason to live in fear of it coming. Although you can't point a finger to the exact day it will happen, you can be sure death is on the horizon. Stay optimistic and focus on the things you can control in the limited time you have on Earth. Chase your passions. Check off new line items on your bucket list every day.

Time is the only capital you can't get back. You can lose money and make more of it, but if you waste time, you will never be able to add another second on the clock. Don't blow the greatest asset you have, and remember, in this sense, you are already rich.

THIRTEEN
STAY IN THE RING

"If you can find a path with no obstacles, it probably doesn't lead anywhere." – Frank A. Clark

"You may not realize it when it happens, but a kick in the teeth may be the best thing in the world for you." – Walt Disney

"There is only one way to happiness and that is to cease worrying about things which are beyond the power of our will." – Epictetus

THE ROCKY ROAD

L ife is nothing but a bunch of consequences. Quality of life is, therefore, a direct result of the actions we take each day in the pursuit of our highest goals. I believe success is ultimately a feeling that boils down to experiencing positive consequences in the areas of life we are most passionate about.

I perceive each new consequence, good or bad, as the result of a significant battle fought, but no single outcome has the power to end the war that will span my entire lifetime. There is no end-all, be-all moment. You will always have another battle to fight, regardless of the wins, losses, or bad press you incur along the way. In other words, the war will continue to rage on until you exhale for the last time. Even when you think you're down for the count, realize that you always have a fighting chance. Claw your way back up and keep pushing on.

As an optimist, I believe the world is an exciting place filled with magnificent highs, but the fact still stands that terrible lows are a part of the experience. Detach emotional pain from your lost battles, they are just consequences of former actions that don't have to define you. Use the losses to become more capable. At the end of the day, when you tally up the consequences of your actions, the goal shouldn't be for strictly plusses across the board, it should be for positive on aggregate. Strive to maintain an upward life trajectory.

Success isn't as much about winning the war as it is about showing up to the fight each day. As long as you don't quit, you can't lose. Failure is a temporary condition. Giving up is permanent. Stay on the rocky road until you make it to the top.

DISCOURAGEMENT, FRUSTRATION, AND WORRY

L ife is a roller coaster. Without the greater perspective that comes with experience, there always seem to be more down moments when you're younger. Young people typically overlook the highs and overemphasize the lows. When I began managing medical laboratories, I spent weeks wondering if I could do anything right. At times, I considered throwing in the towel. These feelings come with the territory. It's normal to feel like this when you fall short in the pursuit of a burning passion, or when you know you aren't where you need to be personally and professionally.

If you feel like you've failed at something, you just figured out that the strategy used was ineffective. You are now one step closer to implementing a solution that will get the job done. Scratch the idea, move down the list, and step back into the ring. Managing discouragement, curbing frustration, and surviving worry is no piece of cake. You must develop endurance and patience, the building blocks of resilience, to succeed. Over time, you will develop the grit to pick yourself up off the bloody canvas each time your body folds and deliver a knock-out counterpunch.

When you feel yourself losing your grip on something in life, or life as whole, it's often a sign that you need to turn back the knob to keep from exploding. A 2019 article written by CNBC's Catherine Clifford revealed that even Bill Gates, the boss of Microsoft, would take a one-week sabbatical two times a year to escape to a secret clapboard cabin somewhere in a cedar forest in the Pacific Northwest. Gates called these solo trips his "Think Week". Clifford goes on to explain how work done during one Think Week eventually led to Microsoft launching Internet Explorer in 1995, as well as many other breakthroughs over the years. Even the ultra successful CEOs of today that breathe a fast-paced, high-stakes lifestyle still feel the urge to get away from it all by cutting off contact with the bustling outside world. They have figured out that life is a tricky balance.

Personally, I've never retreated to complete isolation. At the start of my career, one of my mentors told me if you're not going to be readily available, virtually all the time, you shouldn't get into medicine. I made up my mind that I would always be reachable in order to react quickly to any clinical, patient, or operational problems. Instead of taking week-long breaks, I try not to let too much pressure build up by setting aside time each day to release pent up frustration. I don't believe one way works for all, but that was how I was able to balance stepping away from the madness to catch my breath while still being able to perform my work. It's up to you to find what works best.

Possibly the best advice I can offer to you is this. Don't live life in two-times fast forward. Be present, and put things in proper perspective. Most of what you stress about is insignificant with the passing of time. Earl Nightingale sums up our worries in his timeless classic *Lead the Field*, where he writes,

> According to the Bureau of Standards, "A dense fog covering seven city blocks, to a depth of 100 feet, is composed of something less than one glass of water." So, if all the fog covering seven city blocks, 100 feet deep, were collected and held in a single drinking glass, it would not even fill it. And this could be compared to our worries. If we can see into the future and if we could see our problems in their true light, they wouldn't tend to blind us to the world, to living itself, but instead could be relegated to their true size and place. And if all the things most people worry about were reduced to their true size, you could probably put them all into a drinking glass, too.
>
> It's a well-established fact that as we get older, we worry less. With the passing of the years and the problems each of them yields, we learn that most of our worries are not really worth bothering ourselves about too much and that we can manage to solve the important ones.

But to younger people, they often find their lives obscured by the fog of worry. Yet, here's an authoritative estimate of what most people worry about.

1. Things that never happen: 40 percent. That is, 40 percent of the things you worry about will never occur anyway.
2. Things over and past that can't be changed by all the worry in the world: 30 percent.
3. Needless worries about our health: 12 percent.
4. Petty, miscellaneous worries: 10 percent.
5. Real, legitimate worries: 8 percent. Only 8 percent of your worries are worth concerning yourself about. Ninety-two percent are pure fog with no substance at all.

The feelings of discouragement, frustration, and worry that come with each life challenge won't ever subside, but if you continue to accumulate new experiences, you will become better able to handle the next one.

RUN TOWARD CHALLENGE

P icture this. You inhale a deep breath of pine-scented air from the dense forest surrounding you. It's a steamy spring morning. As you leave your campsite for the day's hike, you spot an enormous black bear searching for something to fill its belly. It can smell you. It turns, elongates on two paws, and lets out a heart-stopping roar. What do you do? For most people, the natural reaction is to run for the hills. However, the minute you take off, the bear will categorize you as prey. Running will trigger the bear's instinct to hunt. A black bear is an excellent climber that can stride out a maximum speed of thirty miles per hour, so unless you have a getaway scooter stashed nearby, you are a goner if you run.

In this situation, your best chance of survival is to rise up as big and tall as you can and roar back at the apex predator. This behavior is called predator-prey reversal. In her scientific report, Predator Prey Role Reversals, Yasuyuki Choh explains that this is a biological interaction where an organism that is typically prey in the predation interaction acts as the predator. By demonstrating that you aren't going to helplessly back down, that you have the teeth to bite back, the bear will perceive you as an apex predator too. After all, you are starting to act like one. Faced with the reality that, even if it succeeds in overwhelming you, it will likely hobble away with scratches and bruises to show for it, in most cases, the wild animal will succumb to its survival instincts and scurry off to find an easier meal.

Throughout your life, you will face many proverbial apex predators that will manifest out of various life challenges. A deadly medical diagnosis, losing a job, a suffocating addiction, painful breakups, divorce, the list goes on. In these situations, most people act like prey, with the natural instinct to play victim by curling up in a ball or running away and hoping the beast will leave them alone.

That is a figment of the imagination. These "predators" will continue to lurk in the shadows and feed on you as long as your back is turned.

A unique pattern among the most successful people I've met is that, instead of fleeing from predatory challenges like prey, they reverse roles and take initiative. They don't waste time spreading blame, taking the situation personally, or feeling sorry for themselves. These professionals have accepted that beastly challenges are inseparable from everyday life, and that they won't dissipate on their own. These individuals rise above their problems, logically working toward solutions with composure and a proactive plan of action, rather than reacting out of rash emotion.

Each day, I'm bombarded with high-stakes, complicated challenges. Conquering them is what keeps my mind and body sharp. They allow me to wake up with purpose, even in old age. Similarly, tough challenges will offer you the unique opportunity to derive a heightened sense of meaning from your life by how you respond to them. I believe challenges are also one of the most powerful drivers of achievement and self-mastery. In this sense, they are something to be grateful for.

This is not to say that dealing with challenges will be a walk in the park. On the contrary, they are often packed with excruciating pain in the present moment. But, by enduring challenges in the short term, you will become a motivated and self-confident individual in the long term. As pressure makes diamonds, challenges make warriors out of average people. It's worth bearing the temporary suffering for what you will become. The irony is that most people spend their time and energy trying to avoid challenging situations. They don't realize that, in doing so, they are sacrificing their future growth. A better alternative would be to stop resisting and exert that same effort into developing a greater ability to handle the stresses and strains that come.

This principle of leaning into challenges will facilitate success in every bucket of your life. Most importantly, it will allow you to constantly expand your comfort zone. Although you will surely make some mistakes in the process, as long as you don't make the same one twice, it's a valuable lesson learned. Gradually, this practice will become easier until it's second nature, but that only comes from facing challenges over and over. You need to get your reps in. You may come to find that what once took all your might to push through doesn't even make you break a sweat anymore. That's accepting a challenge, fighting through it, and using it to grow your ability. It's one of the most powerful role reversals in human nature.

THERE WILL ALWAYS BE SOMETHING

'm board-certified in three disciplines, meaning I've taken residency and the exams in anatomic pathology, clinical pathology, and microbiology, my subspecialty. Couple that with all my practical experience, and you'll understand why I have a unique perspective on the recent COVID pandemic and life in general. The insight I can offer, in the context of what's going on in the world currently, is backed by a decades-long track record spent facing and overcoming similar challenges. To put things in perspective, I grew up during World War II when the tuberculosis outbreak was a deadly threat, lived through the epidemic hemorrhagic fever (EHF) during the Korean War, dealt with influenza in the Cold War era, endured the 1968 H3N2 pandemic that killed over a million people around the time of the Vietnam War, and now I'm maneuvering through COVID and the Russian war in Ukraine alongside you.

Despite the death toll we've incurred these past few years, I still believe two positives can come from this experience. First, this kind of crisis can bring the country together. We are currently in a state of emergency where we have no other choice but to rely on each other for survival, be it as neighbors, friends, family, or coworkers. We've been reawakened to our need for one another. Deeper relationships may blossom out of the rubble.

Second, this experience has reacquainted many people with the hard-knock life. The children and young adults of this generation have been living through an unusual period of economic growth and tremendous technological advancement. Those lacking perspective have come to see this safe, convenient, and prosperous environment as the norm. Many have taken this for granted. Everything was going so well, but life isn't always a bowl of cherries. When the complexion of the world changed overnight, for an indefinite period, it brought people back down to earth. It's a good thing for us to understand our own mortality and that we are still subject to the environment, which can be ruthless. No one is immune to Mother Nature. The panic can unwind people, and some may lose their mind, but I believe the majority will emerge from this more mature.

When we're young, everything seems so easy. At the time, that's life. Anyone who's spent more than a couple decades on this planet knows that isn't always the case. Life is often a backbreaking challenge, but crucial to our evolution. COVID is not only a challenging disease in and of itself. It has sent disruptions rippling through every bucket of our lives, from store closures to job losses to family deaths, to name a few. These additional obstacles have been dumped in front of us, for better or for worse, and they can be powerful catalysts for change. We can use these obstacles to become better people by how we respond.

You've been thrown a monkey wrench; don't sugarcoat it. Some damn thing always happens. Take the wrench, fix what you can, and start positioning yourself for the future after the pandemic. This is the moment to retool and push onward, not to slow your momentum or put your head down. Some people will treat COVID like cement, preventing their progress. Fortunately, for you, this can become an opportunity. Take advantage of the favorable situations created by those who become complacent and choose not to work. Differentiate yourself from the masses. Create your resilient hardworking identity now. Success is a matter of constant adaptation.

A multitude of new opportunities have emerged from this pandemic. Your job is figuring out how to make the most of them. It will undoubtedly require hard work and risk-taking. Carrying the heavy workload of my 9:00 am to 10:00 pm job while trying to design a robust laboratory information system was an exhausting and slow process. Right now, you have one of the same priceless gifts that allowed me to go the distance back then. Youth. Put that incredible energy to use, and you will excel.

As I got older, I started to reflect on my life, but when I was young, going through the ringer, I kept my nose to the grindstone.

I was just trying to get from point A to point B. Looking back, with all the experience and perspective I now have, I probably wouldn't have embarked on many of the risky business and career endeavors I did early on. Conventional limitations remained in my blinders. It was a blessing in disguise that allowed me to create some truly amazing things despite the odds stacked against me. You might be living through this stage of life right now. This is something to get excited about.

Life is never going to stop throwing a barrage of challenging punches at you. There will always be something, whether it's finding your way through a pandemic, making a drastic career move, launching a new company, or overcoming a family emergency. During these once-in-a-lifetime crises, fall back on your library of experience while leveraging the knowledge of successful experts who have more experience than you to stay in the ring, maneuver around the jabs, and win the fight with a series of calculated knockout blows.

AFTERWORDS

AFTERWORDS

It's 6:00 am on a brisk Tuesday morning in San Diego, California. The sun is just beginning to peek over the horizon, shooting orange and pink beams across the winter sky like a Bob Ross painting. I'm sitting at the mahogany desk in my second-floor bedroom, candle lit, tapping away at another chapter of this book. I feel calm and at peace as the wind gently whistles through the cracked-open window. It's quiet for the most part, but I can't help diverting my focus to the myriad chirping birds that zip across the hedges and trees outside. I shut my laptop, lean toward the window, and peer out.

My gaze is fixed on one king palm that seems to reign over all the other foliage with its mighty twenty-foot stature. One single crow caws from the top of its green looping palms while three little brown birds flutter around the magnificent trunk below. A thought jets through my head, "If I was a bird, I'd nest all the way at the top, the safest and premiere vantage point as far as the eye can see."

If you live anywhere other than a dense concrete jungle, you're probably familiar with the symphony of different birds singing at dawn. Depending on where you are in North America, there might be a handful of vireos, flycatchers, orioles, and thrushes all chirping at once, often from the same trees. This is especially apparent in migratory birds feeding in flocks. It raises the question: why don't the birds on the lower parts of the tree, nearer to the dangerous ground floor, try to claim the superior spot on top? I spin back to my desk, open Google and click on an intriguing article that might explain the phenomenon of multiple species of birds coexisting in and around the same trees.

Scott Shalaway, in an article on interspecific competition published in the *Pittsburgh Post-Gazette*, writes, "This violates a basic ecological principle: Two or more species cannot occupy the same niche at the same time, that is, they cannot do the same thing at the same time. The result is competition, and only one species can prevail." He then breaks down a case study on five different species of warblers that live and nest among the same conifer trees in a forest in the northeastern United States. Now, borderline obsessed with finding an answer, I keep reading with my upper body leaning forward, eyes glued to the screen. What the researchers found, upon closer examination of the ecosystem, was that, although they all inhabit the same trees, each species spends different amounts of time in different parts of the trees. They divide the trees up into sections and keep to their own space. Cape May warblers spent the bulk of their time in the highest outermost branches, yellow-rumped warblers in the lower branches, black-throated green warblers in the midsection, Blackburnian warblers in between middle and top, and bay-breasted warblers in the interior branches. Shalaway concludes that, although the five species spend most of their time in the same trees, they minimize competition by using different parts of the trees to find food at different times. Some birds evolved to live lower to the treacherous ground floor while others settled at the cushy top. The fact that all these birds coinhabit the same trees without much competition surprised me initially. I now understand that they do still fight for food and shelter, but, by and large, only among those in the same section of the tree.

All the humans of the world are like the different species of warblers. We all live on planet Earth, but the situation is never equal. One person comes home to a beachfront mansion in Malibu. Another shares a cramped studio in Compton. The same dynamic can be seen in every business organization: some employees play vital roles boasting lucrative compensation packages while others work in the background for meager paychecks far down the organizational tree. This structure is a part of nature. It permeates our society from athletics to career success.

A bird doesn't have the ability to rethink its suboptimal position or take the necessary corrective actions to move up the tree. What is unique to human nature, and differentiates us from other animals, is our ability to consciously choose, each moment, through our life philosophy and subsequent actions, what part of the proverbial tree of life we want to reside on, despite our current position. Our life experience revolves around the choice of where we want to be, and we will remain in the same place surrounded by likeminded individuals until we make a conscious effort to change. This is why some people eat abundantly from life's buffet, living in the highest part of the tree, while others barely get by at the bottom, fighting for the leftover scraps. Although some people might've been born on the top branch, that doesn't mean someone born in the dirt can't rise to the same level. The latter will just have to put in greater effort. This is how those who started at the bottom transformed their lives into the success stories that we marvel over today.

The interesting thing is that the decision of where we want to be, whether we are aware of our answer or not, manifests in the quality of people that surround us. Is it surprising that billionaires befriend and constantly knock other billionaires from their spot on Forbes' list? Or that star athletes train with and against other star athletes? Birds of the same feather flock together. If you want to get in shape, watch what someone in shape does every day, adjust your philosophy, and mirror their actions. Then the unexplainable will start to happen. As you continue to progress, over time, you will naturally start attracting the company of other health-conscious individuals that will accelerate your growth, while falling out of touch with the people that had a detrimental effect on your development. These interactions will pull you closer to your goal like a second wind. It's an incredibly powerful positive feedback loop.

During my time at rock bottom, I felt stagnant, that I would be stuck in my current position as lowest man on the totem pole forever. It shouldn't come as any surprise that my friend group back then had a combined net worth of ninety-nine dollars with the goal of partying and playing video games for a career. At the same time, I hadn't completely given up hope. I was still jealous of and constantly compared myself to both the young millionaires that constantly made headlines in my Instagram feed and some of my close peers who always seemed to be doing better than me. I wanted to be where they were. I just didn't know how or if I was capable of getting there. My jealousy of the individuals who had "made it" tricked me into thinking I was competing with them. This was a misconception. I wasn't even in the same ballgame. I was only in competition with the other boat anchors on the same level as me and, most importantly, with myself. We choose and subsequently adapt to either sink to the bottom or sail at the top. Once we self-select, we no longer compete with anyone below. In fact, we don't do much of anything with them.

I believed I was trapped in place, but those bars were invisible. I just didn't know which way to step to break free. From the depths, when my life nearly ended on a fateful midnight bike ride, to the first conversation I had with Terry, my eyes gradually opened to the reality that I did have the power to free myself. I could change my position in life with deliberate and decisive action. All I had to do was align my philosophy and habits with those who had already achieved the level of success I desired. My life slowly started improving after digesting the winning life approach of someone already thriving at the top, piece by piece.

To pick up where I left off in the Opening Comments, I'm not yet where I need to be, but I'm moving in the right direction. The past few years have been transformative. The ideas in this book are only as valuable as the tangible results they can lead to, and as one of the only individuals that can speak to the power of this complete philosophy, it makes sense to wrap up the story where it all began and mention a few highlights from the year after I graduated college, leading up to my 23rd birthday. At the risk of sounding braggadocious, I ran my first two official half marathons along the Embarcadero in downtown San Diego, finishing in the top 1.6 percent of a pool of 15,000 total competitors. I tried my luck with an Olympic-distance triathlon in Solana Beach, California, and ended up being the first person to cross the finish line. I completed my first 70.3-mile half Ironman in the Southern California desert city of Indian Wells, finishing in the top 25 percent and clocking a total time of less than 5.5 hours. I joined a public bank fresh out of college and originated around $1 billion in commercial real estate loans during my rookie year alongside my small team, leading the company in productivity.

I met my wife-to-be, who grew up in the Midwest of all places. I straightened out my finances and self-funded eleven trips across the continent. I opened a local surf shop. I raised and donated more money the past year than in the last 22 combined, which has helped the 16 Strong Project, a nonprofit, support young adults affected by mental illness due to childhood trauma. If you are reading this, it means I have also published my first book. It seems only fitting that I dove into a completely new industry, just like Terry did. I've had my fair share of downs this past year, although thankfully none of them were bike accidents, but, on balance, I'm in the green.

Although each of these milestones were monumental wins for me, they shouldn't mean anything to you. As Terry would say, you should only compare yourself to the person you were the day before. The point I'm trying to make is that, for the first time, I can actually say I'm proud of how far I've come. This testimonial is only meant to demonstrate that living by the philosophy of someone as proven as Terry really does work. The proof is in the progress.

The irony in all of this is that, before associating with Terry, all I wished for with all my might was for the external circumstances around me to change so that I could improve myself internally. I have since learned that lasting change starts from within. With the help of tested philosophies like Terry's, I was able to cultivate a more positive self-image, boost my confidence, and reach a healthier state of mind. Suddenly, like magic, the external world around me started to come full circle with the utmost ease. I figured out that the inner world dictates the outer world, not the other way around.

I also realized that, although the upward climb seems to be the most painful the closer you are to the ground floor, it is the most exhilarating part of the journey. The goal is to eventually make it to the top, but once you're there, over time, the shine wears off. It's the hard knocks that keep you engaged. What's another million to a multi-millionaire? What's the first million to someone living paycheck to paycheck? Terry taught me that what matters more than the money, or any other gift that awaits me in the future, is the appreciation that I have for myself, for who I'm becoming right now. The fact that I've been down has made me appreciate each step I've since taken in the right direction. The newness of feeling proud of myself has elicited the most potent emotions in my life. Cherish the blessings and struggles that come, they'll make you smile when you're on top. Don't curse your way along like I did.

Hopefully this writing has inspired you to take even the smallest step to change your current trajectory for the better. If you walk away with anything from this book, let it be that change doesn't have to come from you alone. The individuals who have already accomplished what you desire are out there, and they have found the true treasures of life. They are one of the most effective external resources you can leverage to unleash potential within. Between their help and the accumulation of your own personal experience, you will gradually elevate your position on the tree of life and enjoy a heightened state of living.

In case you haven't picked up on it, experience, a word that appears a total of 215 times, is the theme of this book. By chasing it, learning from it, and befriending others that have it, you will be successful at whatever you set out to do. I thank you for reading through to the end. I will now leave you to continue your search for answers. That is, to pick up the next call from experience.

ACKNOWLEDGMENTS

This book grew like an oak tree. It was an extremely slow process. For someone who is notorious for being impatient, this often plagued my mind. One day, call, question, and answer at a time, I pieced this puzzle together. After I had the complete philosophy in front of me and used it to facilitate my own personal transformation, I had a sudden and unrelenting urge to organize this amazing story into something that could be shared with others so they could do the same.

Getting this book across the finish line has been a rocky process over the past few years, as I'm still in the middle of my own evolution in my early twenties. Many fires had to be put out, including entire recorded conversations that mysteriously got deleted, computer viruses that threatened all our digital files, and personal dramas like graduating college and moving to a new city while working full time, which put further strain on our team. These obstacles just about derailed us, but we were resilient. We had to see this through.

First and foremost, I would like to thank Terry for using his little bit of free time to teach me his incredible philosophy. He wore many different hats, from teacher to fact checker to storyteller. Most importantly, he refined my interpretation of his philosophy in great detail, making sure we got it absolutely right.

I would also like to thank my father, a published author and English major, for his guidance throughout the process of writing this book. I would not have wanted to embark on this journey without him. He has a unique ability to add color to words and elicit a humorous flow that can capture the attention of any audience, leaving them with a delightful aftertaste. Without his consistent effort, we would not have been able to cast this message far and wide. Without his suggestion to call someone with experience in the first place, there would have been no story to tell.

Finally, I would like to thank you, the reader, for trusting that we would reward your time with valuable material. Without you, this philosophy would lay dead in its tracks. You inspired me to continue grinding through the late nights when I felt like pulling my hair out, during the months I was faced with writer's block, completely devoid of inspiration, and you were the reason I followed through with publication when the disheartening pressure of insecurities made me consider throwing in the towel. I'm forever grateful for your support. All of us share in the elation of this great success together, and this won't be the last you hear from us. Until next time, we say goodbye.

ABOUT THE AUTHOR

Rory Link is a San Diego native and Del Mar resident. A collegiate soccer player at UC Davis, Link studied economics, technology management, and real estate development. Now he is an Ironman competitor, surf shop owner, licensed real estate professional, and banker. *A Call from Experience* is his first book.

ABOUT THE PUBLISHER

The Sager Group was founded in 1984. In 2012 it was chartered as a multimedia content brand, with the intent of empowering those who create art—an umbrella beneath which makers can pursue, and profit from, their craft directly, without gatekeepers. TSG publishes books; ministers to artists and provides modest grants; and produces documentary, feature, and commercial films. By harnessing the means of production, The Sager Group helps artists help themselves. For more information, please see TheSagerGroup.net.

MORE BOOKS FROM
THE SAGER GROUP

Students Write the Darnedest Things:
Gaffes, Goofs, Blunders and Unintended Wisdom from Actual College Papers
by Pamela Hill Nettleton, PhD

Into the River of Angels: A Novel
by George Wolfe

Meeting Mozart:
A Novel Drawn from the Secret Diaries of Lorenzo Da Ponte
by Howard Jay Smith

Notes from the Road:
A Filmmaker's Journey through American
by Robert Mugge

Going Home to Die No More:
A True Kentucky Story about a Train Robbery and a
Hanging after the Civil War
by Russ Witcher

The Deadliest Man Alive:
Count Dante, The Mob and the War for American Martial Arts
by Benji Feldheim

Lifeboat No. 8: Surviving the Titanic
by Elizabeth Kaye

The Pope of Pot:
And Other True Stories of Marijuana and Related High Jinks
by Mike Sager

See our entire library at TheSagerGroup.net

Artifex Te Adiuva